Bard Press

1515 Capital of Texas Hwy.
Suite 107
Austin, Texas 78746
(512) 329-8373
(512) 329-6051 Fax
www.bardpress.com

Dear Reader:

Some time ago I published a book titled *The Wizard of Ads: Turning Words into Magic and Dreamers into Millionaires*. That collection of essays by Roy Hollister Williams on life and commerce came into my possession under rather extraordinary circumstances, and I felt compelled to share them with a larger audience.

Shortly after the book's publication, correspondence began to pour in from around the country. People in all walks of life told how the Wizard had radically changed the way they thought about advertising, business, and life. Many asked for more help in putting the Wizard's powerful principles into action. His essays had convinced them of the need to change, but the question in their minds was "How?"

One letter mentioned rumors of an Academy, a school of ancient principles and wisdom, where the elusive Wizard shared his philosophy and teachings with selected students. Intrigued, I began to make inquiries, and, after much effort and expense, I was able to verify its existence. My quest eventually brought into my hands the Wizard's annotated teaching guide and numerous personal effects.

The spirit of the Wizard's work best shines through in one of his letters where he says, "There are as many kinds of Wizards as there are passions in the hearts of humanity, yet a single characteristic is common to them all: Wizards love to be fascinated. Refusing to be restricted by the limitations of the body, Isaac Newton, Albert Einstein, and Stephen Hawking attained the status of Wizards of Worlds. Read of Henry Ford and the Wright Brothers and you'll witness the birth of Wizards of Wrenches. Emily Dickinson, Robert Frost, and Dr. Seuss stand in a centuries-long line of Wizards of Words. Teddy Roosevelt, Mother Teresa, and Martin Luther King were Wizards with a Contagious Dream. My question for you is simply this: What kind of Wizard will you be?"

Drawing on the Wizard's teaching guide, here in much of its original form, I offer you this treasure, *Secret Formulas of the Wizard of Ads*. It is my hope, and I'm sure the Wizard's as well, that many future wizards find a personal epiphany within its pages.

Ray Bard
Publisher

Secret Formulas of the Wizard of Ads

Roy H. Williams

Bard Press

Austin

Texas

SECRET FORMULAS OF
the Wizard of Ads

Bard Press
1515 Capital of Texas Highway S., Suite 107
Austin, TX 78746
512-329-8373 voice, 512-329-6051 fax
www.bardpress.com

Ordering Information
To order additional copies, contact your local bookstore or call 800-945-3132.
Quantity discounts are available.
ISBN 1-885167-39-3 trade paperback, 1-885167-40-7 hardcover

Library of Congress Cataloging-in-Publication Data

Williams, Roy H.
    Secret formulas of the wizard of ads / Roy H. Williams.
      p.   cm.
    Includes index.
    ISBN 1-885167-40-7. -- ISBN 1-885167-39-3 (pbk.)
    1. Advertising. I. Title.
HF5823.W496 1999
659.1--dc21
                                          99-16178
                                            CIP

The author may be contacted at the following address:
Roy H. Williams
Williams Marketing, Inc.
1760 FM 967
Buda, TX 78610
512-295-5700 voice, 512-295-5701 fax
www.WizardofAds.com

Credits

Developmental editor: Chris Maddock
Editor: Jeff Morris
Proofreaders: Deborah Costenbader, Letitia Blalock
Index: Linda Webster
Cover design: Suzanne Pustejovsky
Text design/production: Jeff Morris

First printing: July 1999
Second printing: August 1999

Contents

PART THE FIRST: PHILOSOPHY OF ADVERTISING

In Which the Wizard Examines the Question: "What Makes People Do the Things They Do?"

PART THE SECOND: ROOM WITH A VIEW

In Which the Wizard Explains the Functions of the Brain and the Power of Imagination

PART THE THIRD: SIDE DOOR INTO THE MIND

In Which the Wizard Tells You How to Get People to Do What You Want Them to Do

pencil   advertising)

PART THE FOURTH: TURNING LEAD INTO GOLD

In Which the Wizard Explains the Mechanics of Miraculous Ad Writing

PART THE FIFTH: DOING THE HARD THING

In Which the Wizard Offers Advice on Managing a Business

PART THE SIXTH: HOW, THEN, SHOULD WE LIVE?

In Which the Wizard Explains the Art and Science of Life

Part the First

Philosophy of Advertising

**In Which the Wizard Examines the
Question: "What Makes People
Do the Things They Do?"**

1

The Energy of Words

ou study pivotal people and events in history, searching for a common denominator. You hope to identify the recurrent elements of greatness, the keys to phenomenal success. You search for the secret of miracles. After several hundred hours of reading, you reach an utterly inescapable conclusion: Words are the most powerful force there has ever been.

Monumental events explode with energetic words, and great leaders are remembered for the things they say. Although a grand idea may carry the seeds of change, it takes powerful words to launch the idea skyward, words strong enough to carry the full weight of vision. Likewise, great ad campaigns begin with grand ideas and come alive with vivid words.

Oddly enough, most business people have fabulous ideas; they simply don't have the words. Their wonderful ideas are sadly short-circuited when they cannot find the words to carry them skyward.

You have seen Rodin's famous sculpture *The Thinker* and were intrigued the moment you saw it. But how your interest increases when you hear Rodin speak of it! "What makes my Thinker think is that he thinks not only with the brain, with his knitted brow, his distended nostrils, and compressed lips, but with every muscle of his arms, back, and legs; with his clenched fist and gripping toes." Seeing it now with our ears, we find Rodin's *Thinker* far more interesting than when we saw it only with our eyes.

Words are electric; they should be chosen for the emotional voltage they carry. Weak and predictable words cause grand ideas to appear so dull that they fade into the darkness of oblivion. But powerful words in unusual combinations brightly illuminate the mind.

Yes, words are electric. If a sentence does not shock a little, it carries no emotional voltage. When the hearer is not jolted, you can be sure he is not moved. Remember the words of Napoleon: "Small plans do not inflame the hearts of men."

Words start wars and end them, create love and choke it, bring us to laughter and joy and tears. Words cause men and women willingly to risk their lives, their fortunes, and their sacred honor. Our world, as we know it, revolves on the power of words.

In your ads, use words that are majestic, words that have the power to inflame people's hearts and illuminate their minds.

Words are, of course, the most powerful drug used by mankind.

Rudyard Kipling

2

Specifics and Generalities

It's 2 AM and my friend Tony and I have walked 270 feet down a dark alley to the back of a hardware store, then turned around to see a policeman standing next to our car. We stare at each other a moment, then slowly walk the 270 feet back toward the policeman. I tell Tony, "Don't say a word. Let me handle it. You'll just get us cuffed and scuffed." I turn to the cop.

"Hello officer I'm sure this looks suspicious but my name is Roy Hollister Williams and this is my best friend Anthony Marc White and we were having an argument in the kitchen of my house at two-eleven West Detroit where my wife Pennie is in bed already because she can't stay awake past ten o'clock and Tony said he was thinking about renting this vacant space next to the hardware store for an auto body shop because he thinks he can get twenty cars in this place and I said No way because the building is barely a hundred and fifty feet long and he said it was twice that long so we bet a cheeseburger and then came here to step it off together and I'm really good at stepping off distances because I used to work as an estimator for Aqua-Tite Seamless Guttering Company on Mingo Road and I can step off any distance to the exact foot because I used to do it several times a day to estimate the length of the guttering because we sold it by the foot and I had to bid the jobs and — "

"He's gone," says Tony. "You can quit babbling like an idiot now."

"Yeah," I answer, "but at least we're not in jail. Every time you talk to a cop, everyone within fifty feet of you goes to jail, and while that might sound like fun, I've got to go to work in the morning."

"Okay," says Tony, "but you still owe me a cheeseburger."

Even though I'm only twenty, I already know that specifics are more believable than generalities. Tonight it saves me from taking a long ride in the back seat of a patrol car, and tomorrow it will help me write the kinds of ads that make people rich. In another few years, I'll use this little nugget of insight to launch my own advertising firm.

The simple truth is that nothing sounds quite so much like the truth as the truth, and most people seem to know the truth when they hear it. The truth is never full of loopholes and generalities. The truth is made of specifics and substantiation; it's solid. That's why it's easy to spot in a world full of paper-thin lies, half-lies, and hype.

What about your ads? Are they full of generalities and unsubstantiated claims? If so, your customer probably thinks you're lying even when you're telling the truth. Ads that sound like "ads" are never quite convincing.

Do your ads sound like "ads"?

A cliché is a truth one doesn't believe.

Bernard Taper

3

Dead Cows Everywhere

Rarely do ad campaigns work as well as they should. I blame the three sacred cows of advertising: demographic targeting, gross rating points, and media mix. I think it's time for these cows to die.

Demographic targeting tells us that success can be found by "reaching the right people." Consequently, advertisers focus on targeting and discount the importance of saying the right thing. In truth, decisions are seldom made in a vacuum. Each of us is influenced by a host of friends, relatives, co-workers, and strangers. The true secret of advertising success is to say the right thing to as many people as you can afford to reach over and over again. Word-of-mouth advertising is the result of having impressed someone, anyone, deeply.

Gross rating points tell us that persuading 100 percent of the city 10 percent of the way will work just as well as convincing 10 percent of the city 100 percent of the way. Those who buy gross rating points nearly always reach too many people with too little repetition.

See ch. 57, "The Goose and the Gander."

Media mix tells us that the same people who see your newspaper ads will also hear your radio ads and notice your billboards. Media mix further assumes that the customer will recognize all these as having come from the same advertiser. Yet rarely is one of these fragmented campaigns connected in the mind of the consumer.

Has the time come to replace the three sacred cows of advertising? Yes, I believe it has, and as you read ahead, you'll understand what I'm talking about.

4

Uniquely Unqualified

In one critical respect, the advertising business is unlike any other. The idea that the customer is always right may be true in every other business, but it will lead an advertising person to ruin just as surely as if he had jumped off a cliff. The ad writer who believes the client is always right will give the client what he requests instead of what he really needs. Everything will be roses in the short run, but when the campaign yields disappointing results, the ad person will get all the blame for the client's bad idea.

People in business are uniquely *un*qualified to see their own companies and products objectively. Too much product knowledge causes them to instinctively answer questions no one is asking. This makes for extremely ineffective advertising. A few years ago, Pennzoil spent millions of dollars shouting to America, "Pennzoil is the only leading brand of motor oil to meet the 1996 S.A.E. requirements two years early." I'm still looking for the person they thought might care.

Never take the advice of an advertising person who is quick to agree with you. The first rule of every good ad consultant is this: The customer is always wrong.

Advertising may be the only business in the world where the clients with the most money can make demands until they get the agency's worst product, while the small client with little to spend must meekly accept the agency's best.

Thomas D. Murray

5

Selling the Inside Champion

As a little kid, I watched a clown named Ronald launch a worldwide fast-food empire by winning the hearts of "inside champions" all across America. Ronald found his champions watching Saturday morning cartoons, and he impressed them with the idea that a toy should be included with the purchase of every hamburger and fries. Ronald knew that each little inside champion rode in the back seat of a car driven by a decision maker and that when the time came for that decision maker to make a decision, his inside champion would spring into action.

I've warned you not to fall into the trap of thinking you must target "the decision maker" in your advertising, but in reality, our irrational tendency to overtarget becomes even more pronounced in face-to-face selling situations. Perhaps it's because sales trainers have long insisted that the first step in making a sale is to reach the decision maker: "Don't waste time on people who have no authority." The result of this horrible advice has been that salespeople habitually ignore the friendly and readily accessible inside champions who could make the job of selling so incredibly easy — the secretary, the file clerk, the husband, the wife, the golfing buddy, or the friend of a friend.

See ch. 3, "Dead Cows Everywhere."

But never try to target an inside champion! (No one likes being "used.") Just realize that inside champions are all around you, every day. All you need to do is tell your very convincing and compelling story to anyone and everyone who will listen to it. You never know who a person might know.

While it has always been difficult to reach the person who has final authority to make a decision, reaching all the people around that person is usually incredibly easy. And if even one of these people is deeply impressed with your story, what do you think is going to happen? Especially if you haven't asked that person to talk to the boss for you? Remember: It's not who you reach, it's what you say that counts. Or as my friend Rich Mann says, "It's not who you know, it's who knows you."

How many strangers do you impress with your story each day? Have you been ignoring all the friendly, powerful inside champions that surround you? Have you mistakenly assumed that they couldn't help you because they weren't decision makers?

Are you proud of the product or service you sell? If so, then talk about it! Even if the people who are listening all seem to be small potatoes.

See "overtargeting," p. 123.

6

b' b' b' Bennie and the Jets

I'm standing on an island in New York Harbor, quietly gazing up at the torch of Lady Liberty, when my ears catch a distant rumble. The noise quickly becomes a rushing roar, and for an instant the pale blue sky above the Lady's torch turns dark as six navy jets pass over her in tight formation. It's the first time I've ever seen the Blue Angels. My thoughts turn immediately to Bennie.

Bennie is a printer who has taught his craft to several young people, then helped each one of them open his own little printing shop. Bennie remains a silent partner in each of the shops as he sells his young partners all their paper and printing supplies. Most people think Bennie is a printer, but in reality, Bennie is a salesman.

Bennie is such a good salesman, in fact, that he has been sent to make an impossible sale. His employers need money desperately, but no one is willing to loan it to them because everyone knows they are going under. Bennie's mission is to secure the funding that will allow them to survive, an amount totaling several million dollars, and Bennie has nothing to offer as collateral. But Bennie has a plan.

Bennie wangles himself an invitation to a dinner party where movers and shakers will be gathered, but instead of smiling and handing his business card to each of the powerful men, Bennie slips into the room next door where all the men's wives have gathered. Bennie smiles and listens and asks perceptive questions and is soon quite a favorite among the ladies, so it comes as no surprise when he is invited to party after party. And each time it is the same: speak with the women, avoid the men.

One night, the ladies say, "Bennie, tell us about yourself. Tell us about where you are from." Soon they are spellbound as Bennie speaks from his heart about his employers and their lofty goals, hopes, dreams, and beliefs. Within a few days, Bennie's employers have the money they need.

As the Blue Angels pass over Lady Liberty, my mind turns to Bennie, because this is the statue that was sent as a gift to Bennie's employers by the nice people who loaned them the money back in 1777. It was during America's darkest hour that Benjamin Franklin arranged to borrow from France the money needed to continue the Revolutionary War. One hundred years later, the French congratulated Bennie's employers on their success with a little gift called the Statue of Liberty.

Fortunately for America, Bennie knew how to win the hearts of inside champions, and it helped him save a struggling young nation. So tell me, would there be a statue in New York Harbor today if Bennie had been trained to deal only with decision makers? 🙶

See ch. 5, "Selling the Inside Champion."

Every man has two countries and one of them is France.

Benjamin Franklin

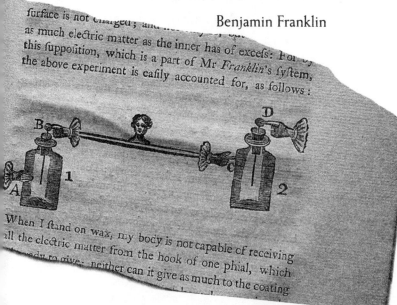

7

What Is Branding?

"Branding" is the hot new buzzword favored by smooth-talking ad people who always seem to speak as though it were something new and mysterious. I have yet to find even one of these empty suits who has the slightest idea of how branding is accomplished in the mind.

Branding is far from new. Ivan Pavlov won a Nobel prize for his research into branding in 1904. Remember the story? Day after day, Pavlov would ring a bell as he rubbed meat paste onto the tongue of a dog. The dog soon began to associate the taste of the meat with the sound of the bell until salivation became the dog's conditioned response. In psychological terms, this is implanting an associative memory — in other words, "branding," in its full glory.

There are three keys to implanting an associative memory into the mind of your customer. The first key is consistency. Pavlov never offered food without ringing the bell, and he never rang the bell without offering food. The second key is frequency, meaning that Pavlov did it day after day after day.

The third key, anchoring, is the tricky one. When an associative memory is being implanted, the new and unknown element (the bell) has to be associated with a memory that's already anchored in the mind (the taste of meat). Frequency and consistency create branding only when your message is tied to an established emotional anchor. Pavlov's branding campaign was anchored to the dog's love for the taste of meat. If the dog did not love meat, the frequent and consistent ringing of the bell would have produced no response other than to irritate the dog.

If I say, "It's a Norman Rockwell kind of restaurant," you immediately think of the place as being cozy, happy, warm, innocent, and

Branding: The implantation of an associative memory in combination with a recall cue.

kid-friendly, right? Your assumptions about the restaurant are anchored to your feelings about the art of Norman Rockwell. If I frequently and consistently cause you to associate the restaurant with Norman Rockwell, I am implanting an associative memory into your mind — branding.

The buying public is your dog. If you desire a specific response from it, you must tie your identity to an emotional anchor that's already known to elicit the desired response. If you make such an association consistently and frequently, branding will occur. But don't expect too much too soon. It takes a lot of repetition to train the dog to salivate at the sound of your name.

Do you have the patience, Pavlov? 🦎

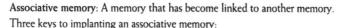

Associative memory: A memory that has become linked to another memory.

Three keys to implanting an associative memory:

1. Consistency
2. Frequency
3. Anchoring

Anchoring: When implanting an associative memory, the recall cue must be associated with a memory that is already anchored in the mind. Frequency and consistency create "branding" only when your message is tied to an established emotional anchor.

Recall cue: A mental trigger that prompts a reader/listener/viewer to take a prescribed action at an appointed time. Often (incorrectly) called a reticular activator. The probability of recalling the associates of a cue diminishes with the number of possible associations. The fewer things a word can mean, the better it will function as a recall cue.

Recently, I was seated on a plane next to a marketing executive from a large company. She told me that her company's new $14 million "branding" campaign was built upon the consistent use of the same three colors in all their brochures and magazine ads.

I predict that this woman will soon be waving goodbye to her money as it drifts away on the tide. With fourteen million on the line, I think I might have tied it to a stronger anchor!

8

Category Dominance

The ultimate goal of branding is to establish category dominance — to become the company that customers think of immediately and the one they feel best about whenever your product category is named.

Toys "R" Us is currently category dominant in toys, Home Depot in home improvement products, and Circuit City in electronic appliances, while Staples, Office Depot, and Office Max are slugging it out to see who will be category dominant in office supplies. Though each of these is a superstore, category dominance is not really about square footage at all. It's about courage.

Can you imagine his friends' response when Harland Sanders announced that he was going to open a restaurant serving nothing but fried chicken? "You're gonna do whaaaaat? You're gonna go broke, is what you're gonna do! Not everybody likes chicken, and those who do don't want to eat it every day! Let's say eight people are ridin' in a car and seven of 'em want chicken, but the eighth person doesn't like chicken. What's he supposed to do, wait in the car? Servin' nothin' but chicken is about as smart as havin' a plumbing company that does nothin' but open clogged drains, or a havin' a giant store full of nothin' but toys. You're gonna go broke, Colonel. You're definitely goin' broke."

With nothing but a pressure cooker and eleven secret herbs and spices, Harland Sanders launched Kentucky Fried Chicken, and it became an American institution. Likewise, Starbucks Coffee and Radio Shack achieved category dominance with only a few square feet and relatively few dollars in inventory. Category dominance can be achieved only through focus with commitment. Will you be category dominant? If so, you must take a stand and be known for something.

What will you be known for? 🙠

9

Who Is Your Customer?

ach and every day, ten thousand advertising salespeople ask ten thousand business owners, "Who is your customer?" and the business owners reply, "Blah, blah, blah." Then the ad rep says, "What a coincidence! That's exactly who we reach!" The business owner then buys the advertising because he wants to "target" the right people.

This is precisely how most advertising is bought and sold. (Don't be embarrassed that you've done it, because I've done it, too.)

Unfortunately, this business owner has been asked a largely irrelevant question and has replied with an equally irrelevant answer. What the business owner has done is known as "overtargeting," and it's what invariably happens when advertising is approached from the perspective of pure logic.

Here's why the perfectly logical approach so often fails: We'll assume the business owner decides his target is a woman between twenty-five and fifty-four years of age. Do we now assume that the woman has no parents or siblings? Has she no mate, children, or boyfriend? Does she utterly lack co-workers and associates, neighbors and friends? Is she influenced by no one at all?

See "overtargeting," p. 123.

Overtargeting comes from the mistaken assumption that people make decisions in a vacuum. The really important question to answer is this: "Why would a person choose to do business with you at all?"

The best ads are those that impress someone — anyone — deeply. Are you ensuring that your ads make a deep impression, or are you satisfied in knowing that you're boring the socks off all the "right" people? 🐜

10

Good Ol' Hamp Baker!

Not old enough to drive, I sit in the back seat and read billboards for 200 miles. What else can a fourteen-year-old kid do to pass the time? Outside my window, Hereford cattle stand behind barbed wire fences looking every bit as bored as I feel.

We've traveled less than thirty miles before I'm yawning and thinking, "Herefords all look alike, and most billboards are just oversized yellow-page ads." But wait, what's this? The crumpled hood of an old car leans against a barbed wire fence. Spray painted on the hood, a message: "Hamp Baker Says Drive with Care."

Who the heck is Hamp Baker?

Near Bristow, a wrecked '62 Chrysler sits in a pasture. Along its length, the message, "Hamp Baker Says Drive with Care." All the way from Tulsa to Ardmore, Hamp Baker expresses his concern for my well-being, and I'm not the only one who notices. Within months, he's a statewide mystery.

Later that year, on election day, I'm sitting in a folding chair in the school cafeteria, waiting for my mom to do her patriotic duty. I hear a woman laugh. A few minutes later, a man guffaws and I see that everyone who emerges from behind the curtain is smiling. When Mom comes out, she tells me that listed among the unknowns in the obscure race for corporation commissioner is our old traveling buddy, Hamp Baker.

He wins by a landslide.

Perhaps he just didn't have the money to post billboards that said, "Hamp Baker for Corporation Commissioner," but I prefer to believe he was a marketing genius. I think Hamp Baker knew full well that no one really cared who served as corporation commissioner and that most voters would simply mark the name that felt right.

It's been decades since Hamp Baker was elected, and not once in all those years have I spoken to anyone who ever actually met the man or knew anything at all about him. Yet thirty years after he spray-painted a few dozen cars with his message of warmth and concern, thousands of Oklahomans continue to smile whenever they hear his name. I believe Hamp Baker instinctively understood the power of associative memory: "Win the heart, and the mind will follow." Who knows how high he might have climbed if he had set his sights a little higher?

Drive with care.

See "associative memory," p. 23.

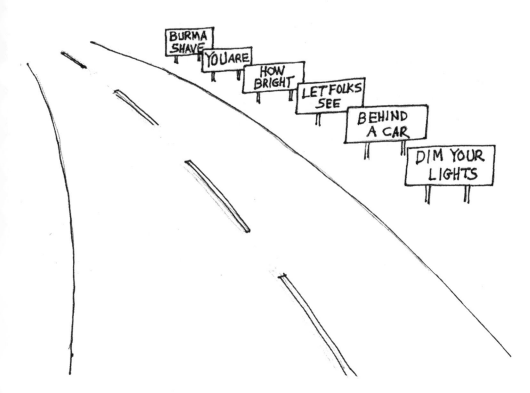

11

Digging for the Diamond

There is a story that is uniquely and wonderfully your own, but you'll never uncover it by trying to imitate the success of others. When digging for the diamond that is your own unique selling proposition, you'll have to sift through a lot of worthless dirt before you find a single nugget of radiant truth. But in the end, it's worth it.

Don't be discouraged. Dig for the diamond. Find the story that is uniquely and wonderfully your own, then tell that story with every ounce of your being.

Unique selling proposition (USP): The message you deliver to a prospective customer that distinguishes you from your competitors and makes the customer want to buy from you.

A lion survives by being a lion, and a mouse, by being a mouse.

Martin Landau to Matt Damon
in *The Rounders* (Miramax Films)

12

Money, a Name, and a Difference

People who begin their questions with "Would it work if . . . " are always the easiest ones for me to answer, because my answer never changes: "Yes, it might 'work' if you did that — but would it be the highest and best use of the money?"

The next question is all too predictable: "Well, then, what would be the highest and best use of the money?" And again, my answer never changes, but it's not because I'm trying to dodge the question or want to play silly games. The only honest way to answer this question is to ask the questioner, "How do you plan to measure success?"

Pennie tells me, "Everyone wants to make the same three things: money, a name, and a difference. What creates diversity in the human race is how we prioritize the three." There's really no right way or wrong way to prioritize the three, though how you do so will radically impact your ad strategy. The highest and best use of your ad budget is essentially determined by your heartfelt answer to a single question:

What is it that you most want to make — money, a name, or a difference?

It is the hopes and dreams that we have that make us great.

13

Seeing Your Customer Real

I've been paid a small fortune to come to Palm Beach, Florida, because some equipment manufacturers are very frustrated with their advertising, and they've flown in from all across America in search of help. I'm training the group on the core principles of effective advertising when one of them raises his hand to say, "These concepts may be valid for advertising to retail customers, but our products are sold to businesses. This stuff might sell ice cream and bicycles and jewelry and clothing, but business-to-business advertising is different."

"Oh, really?" I smile. "Do your customers not buy ice cream and bicycles and jewelry and clothing? Do they magically appear each morning at nine, then vanish into thin air at five? Do they have no secret hopes or dreams? Are they as empty of life as you seem to believe? Are your customers truly the one-dimensional beings you describe?"

Fortunately for me, my listeners possess the wisdom and humility to accept their need of a new perspective, so they're not offended by my blunt challenge of their flawed logic. Here's what I tell them:

"The single greatest mistake made by most advertisers today is that they fail to see their customers real."

Few advertisers see themselves and their customers as complete human beings. This is a failure mostly of insight. Though you may pretend otherwise, you are the same person at work that you are at home. There is no magical change of identity that occurs while you are in transit.

Many of my friends, clients, and associates have asked, "Why do you tell so many stories that have nothing to do with business? Why don't you talk more about advertising?" In truth, I write about life beyond business because your customers have a life beyond business, your employees have a life beyond business, and you have a life beyond business. I write in the hope that you will come to see yourself and your staff and your customers real.

See ch. 60, "Seeing Yourself Real."

When you've learned to do it, your business will grow — not by percentages, but by multiples.

Tell the story that is uniquely and wonderfully your own.

14

The Changing Face of the Rich

What do the rich worry about? Current trends are perhaps best summarized in a recent survey conducted by Financial Market Research for U.S. Trust, a New York–based company specializing in asset management, private banking, and securities services.

In a survey of "baby boomers" (1) between the ages of thirty-one and forty-nine, (2) in the top 1 percent of wealthiest Americans, and (3) with household income over $200,000 or net worth greater than $3 million, 56 percent are concerned about losing their jobs or going out of business, 69 percent fear they won't have enough money to ensure a comfortable retirement, and 71 percent worry about maintaining their income. To cut back on costs, this top 1 percent of the baby boomers typically own just one home and rarely buy jewelry or fine art.

The survey concludes by saying, "These findings fly in the face of the common perception left over from the 1980s that wealthy baby boomers are conspicuous consumers devoted to spending on themselves."

So what are the rich doing with their time and money? According to researchers Kevin Clancy and Robert S. Shulman, the trend among the wealthy today is toward "personal, customized, individual accomplishments — writing a book, climbing Mount Everest, learning Japanese."

Clancy and Shulman go on to say, "Our research has found a need for deeper social connections, particularly with one's family; a need for greater emotional enhancement; a desire for more meaningful social commitments and community involvement; and living what is increasingly called a 'self-examined' life."

Other research indicates that most Americans are starved for leisure time — for having time to do things by themselves, for themselves, or with their families. Almost half of all Americans feel they have little or no free time. More than two-thirds would like to slow down and live a more relaxed life, while only one in five would prefer to live a more exciting, faster-paced life.

"So," you ask, "what are you trying to tell us?"

I'm merely pointing out that the felt needs of society are changing, and the kinds of ads that worked yesterday probably won't work as well today or at all tomorrow. I want you to understand the new flavor you will detect in the ads you see tomorrow and in years to come. I want you to be able to make some sense out of it. 🌿

Try not to become a man of success, but rather a man of value.

Albert Einstein

15

Out of Style

ob is sneering at my English tweed sport coat with the suede patches on the elbows. He says, "You know that jacket's been out of style for about a decade, don't you?"

I answer him with the truth: "Yeah, Bob, I know it's out of style. That's why I wear it." Bob has known me for a long time, but he still hasn't figured out that "out of style" is my style.

"Style" is the unmistakable mark of a follower, and those who are constrained by it are destined to be forever average. Followers always fear breaking the unwritten rules.

Unwritten rules abound in the advertising business, and the foremost of these is "Never put the client in the ad." Any ad firm who puts the client in an ad is certain to be criticized as having done it "only because the client likes to hear himself on the radio and see himself on TV." The people who voice these accusations the loudest, though, are the creators of those highly polished but horribly ineffective "professional" ads that win all the Ad Club awards.

It's always been out of style for business owners to speak on behalf of their own companies, yet Harland Sanders (KFC), Lee Iacocca (Chrysler), Dave Thomas (Wendy's), and George Zimmer (Men's Wearhouse) achieved fantastic success as a direct result of their willingness to ignore the dictates of style. They were unwilling to follow the rules and create ads that were only average.

There was something magical about Lee Iacocca facing the camera and saying to America, "If you can find a better car, buy it." His resolute audacity saved the jobs of tens of thousands of Chrysler employees. That same magic happens every time George Zimmer looks into the lens and says, "You're going to like the way you look. I guarantee it."

How about you? Are you willing to look the world in the eye and tell your story with confidence? Do you fear what people will say if you become the spokesperson for your company? Yes, if you do it, I promise that you will be criticized. The average person will snicker and ridicule you behind your back.

But then again, he's only average.

Good advertising is no guarantee of success;
nor does bad advertising always mean failure.

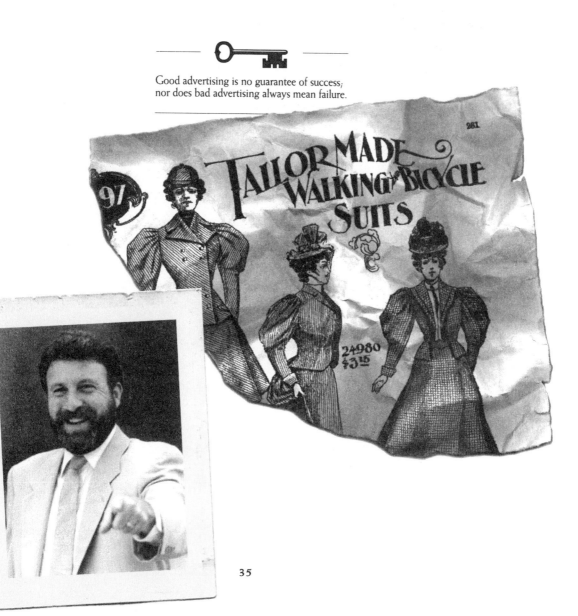

16

You Meet the Most Interesting People

Subject: Subscribe MMM

Date: Sat, 30 Jan 1999 08:13:46 -0500

From: "JIM HUEBNER" <JHUEBNER@PACKET.NET>

To: "Roy Williams" <roy@rhw.com>

Hello;

Up until I read "The Wizard of Ads" the most defining moment in my life was when I stood on the summit of Alaska's Mt. McKinley--the tallest mountain in North America.

But now I have to add reading "The Wizard Of Ads."

For awhile I was involved with a full-blood Ute Indian gal. Her natural beauty is soooooooo stunning that men don't just look at her--they stop what they're doing to look at her.

Well, that's what I did when I got my copy of "The Wizard of Ads." I stopped everything I was doing and read it cover to cover.

And like reaching the summit of Mt. McKinley, if you've never read "The Wizard Of Ads" you can't imagine it. But when you do--you'll never forget it.

Sign me up for MMM. Thanks.

Jim Huebner

Subject: What can I say?
Date: Sat, 30 Jan 1999 09:27:09 +0000
From: "Roy Williams" <roy@rhw.com>
Organization: Roy H. Williams Marketing
To: "JIM HUEBNER" <JHUEBNER@PACKET.NET>

Jim,

Wow. What can I say? Though we receive hundreds of letters and e-mails each month, I've never received one the equal of yours.... I even hesitate to write you this note, for fear that it won't live up to your expectations.

By the way, what the heck were you doing on the top of Mt. McKinley?

Roy H. Williams

Subject: Top of Mt. McKinley
Date: Sat, 30 Jan 1999 15:42:15 -0500
From: "JIM HUEBNER" <JHUEBNER@PACKET.NET>
To: "Roy Williams" <roy@rhw.com>

Howdy there Roy;

You asked me what I was doing on the top of Mt. McKinley--well, I was 50 years old and I was finding out (and accepting) the truth about myself.

FYI: Here are Jim's 6 Rules of Mountaineering (and I think they could also apply to advertising).

1. Climb with passion.
2. No guts, no glory.
3. Expect dead ends.

4. Never turn your back on your partner.

5. Never look where you don't want to go.

6. There's always room on the rope for a person with honor.

What attracts me to mountaineering is that it's very simple: you either live or you die. No time-out, no substitutions, no half-time, no 2-minute warning. And the mountain doesn't care what kind of car you drive, what kind of watch you wear, what college you went to or how much $$$$ you make. Mountaineering is a very "in the moment" experience. And it's one of only two things I've found in my life where, on a consistent basis, doing it is far more exciting than the anticipation of doing it.

What do you think the other one is? Most people say "Sex." No, it's not sex (remember, I said, "on a consistent basis"). The second is speed--going fast. You can never anticipate the feeling of speed.

Roy, be good to yourself.

Jim

There is a fine line between bravery and stupidity. If you get away with it, you are brave. If you don't, you are stupid.

Francisco T. Escario

17

The Wizard Who Got Away

After speaking to a rapt audience for nearly an hour, Frank smiles and says, "Thank you for letting me be with — " but the rest of his words are drowned in thunderous applause as his listeners leap to their feet in ovation. Stepping back from the lectern, Frank smiles and mutters, "Thank you, thank you." Then he sees a hand raised at the back of the room. "Yes, do you have a question?"

A distinguished gentleman steps into the aisle and the crowded room grows quiet. With one eyebrow arched imperiously he scans the room, then looks at Frank and says, "Although I appreciate the personal philosophies you've shared with us this afternoon, certainly a man in your profession must recognize the value of solid facts and hard science." Pausing to let the full impact of his statement ripple across the room, the man delivers a second, stinging jab, "Why has no reputable university embraced your theories?" After another brief pause, "Why haven't you been asked to speak at Harvard?"

Smiling, Frank replies instantly, "Harvard? Harvard takes perfectly good plums as students, and turns them into prunes." Bursts of stifled laughter break out across the room.

The man in the aisle retorts, "But the facts! You speak as though there were things more important than the facts!"

With a smile more sympathetic than mocking, Frank gazes at the man as though the two of them were the only ones in the room and quietly says, "The truth is more important than the facts."

I have been told the applause still echoes in that room.

Frank's instinctive grasp of complex relationships and his unique ability to find beauty in even the most ordinary places would have made him one of the greatest ad writers of all time. But Frank Lloyd

Wright was not energized by the music of words; his artistic rhythm pulsed to the beat of concrete and steel. "Every great architect is — necessarily — a great poet," he said. "He must be a great original interpreter of his time, his day, his age."

Like every great ad writer, Frank shunned "one size fits all" solutions and steadfastly refused to begin a building's design until he had first explored the building site

Frank Lloyd Wright designed buildings in his head, later committing them to paper for clients and contractors. When Edgar Kaufmann arrived unexpectedly in Madison, Wisconsin, and phoned that he was driving to Taliesin to see the plans for his house, Wright sat down at a drafting table and, in 140 minutes, filled sheet after blank sheet with the plans for what became known as Fallingwater, considered by many to be the most influential house of the 20th century. Finishing his work just as Kaufmann entered, he stood and said, "I've been waiting for you."

and met the people who would occupy it. Had he chosen to become a writer instead of an architect, I feel certain that his ad campaigns would have been as uniquely tailored as his buildings, and I believe that he would have moved us with ads we did not even recognize to be ads. Frank also seems to have had an intuitive understanding of the nine secret words.* "Early in life," he says, "I had to choose between honest arrogance and hypocritical humility. I chose honest arrogance and have seen no occasion to change."

Though he never penned a single word of advertising, Frank Lloyd Wright remains a legend among the wizards of ads, who know him simply as "The One Who Got Away."

*"The risk of insult is the price of clarity."
— The Wizard of Ads

No house should ever be on any hill or on anything. It should be of the hill, belonging to it, so hill and house could live together each the happier for the other.

Frank Lloyd Wright

Part the Second

Room with a View

In Which the Wizard Explains
the Functions of the Brain
and the Power of Imagination

18

Living with Tarzan in the Jungle

If the ratio of sensory receptors to brain synapses is any indication, then you and I are comparatively ill equipped to experience a material world. Though our 100 million sensory receptors enable us to see, hear, feel, taste, and smell the real world, our 10,000 billion brain synapses allow us to relate new data to stored memories and ideas — to experience things that never happened.

Yes, reality is a fragile thing. We are much better equipped for experiences that are contained fully in the mind. We have lived with Tarzan in the jungle, journeyed beneath the sea with Captain Nemo, been stranded on an island with Robinson Crusoe, and sailed with a peg-legged man named Ahab as he pursued a great white whale. If these experiences were the only evidence of our amazing abilities, they would surely be enough. But wait, there's more.

A teenage prodigy named Ludwig van Beethoven met the great Wolfgang Amadeus Mozart just a few years before Mozart died. Not yet old enough to shave, Beethoven was already swimming in fame and recognition. His compositions were solicited by publishers before they were even finished. Yet in less than a decade, young Beethoven was struggling with thoughts of suicide. Our young musical genius had begun to lose his hearing.

Beethoven chose to live, however, and to continue his work as a composer, though as he became increasingly deaf, his works became more difficult to understand. It was during his years of total deafness that he answered a critic by saying, "They are not for you, but for a later age."

Had Beethoven been able only to maintain the quality of his compositions during his years of total deafness, most people would have considered it an amazing feat. Yet Beethoven did not merely equal his earlier compositions, he greatly surpassed them. The complex and magical things he wrote while living in a world of utter silence are generally considered to be his greatest masterpieces.

Ludwig van Beethoven was capable of hearing music in a silent world, but his ability to hear symphonies in his head was nothing special. Beethoven's brain was no more capable than those of the people with whom you deal every day. Physiologically, each of us is Beethoven's equal. You can hear Beethoven's *Fifth Symphony* in your mind right now, if you'd like. Remember how it begins?

Just like you and me and Ludwig, your customers have the amazing ability to see with their eyes closed and to hear when there is no sound. They can touch what isn't there and taste what they have not yet eaten. In your advertising, don't speak to the world outside your customers, speak to the world inside their minds. Give them a taste of the experience you have waiting for them in this meeting place we call Reality.

See "iconic memory," "echoic memory," p. 55.

Engage the imagination, then take it where you will. Where the mind has repeatedly journeyed, the body will surely follow. People go only to places they have already been in their minds.

The Wizard's Seventh Law of the Advertising Universe

19

Imagination and Sympathy

dam Smith believes that imagination and sympathy are the keys to understanding one's place in the world. Adam says that imagination lets us become impartial spectators of our own lives. According to Adam, we instinctively use our imagination to put ourselves in the position of others so that we might judge our actions as they will: "What will people think?" Sympathy then lets us predict how others will feel about the actions we're considering. Adam says we make most decisions this way.

Adam Smith could have become rich in advertising. Unfortunately, he was born in deep poverty in Kirkcaldy, Scotland, in 1723, fifty-three years before Thomas Jefferson penned America's Declaration of Independence and thirty-six years after Isaac Newton first demonstrated the law of universal gravitation. Advertising wasn't much of a career back then.

According to Adam, it was Isaac Newton's discovery that caused him to wonder if analogous laws might be at work in human society. Adam Smith asked himself a fundamental question: "What makes people do the things they do?" Specifically, he was concerned with the fate of common people; he wanted to help them. Adam's father had died when he was an infant, and he spent most of his life worrying about the fate of "Momma Smith" and thousands of others like her. His singular dream and goal was to help create an economy that would produce "opulence" for the common folk. Adam Smith wanted his Momma to have a better life.

At age fifty-three, Adam published a work that he had been writing for seventeen years: *An Inquiry into the Nature and Causes of the Wealth of Nations.* The year was 1776. Momma Smith passed away before Adam's dream could find a home, but a certain Thomas Jefferson would later call Adam Smith "the master of those who write about political economy."

You may not hear it taught in history class, but the simple truth is that the American Dream was born in the heart of a poor Scottish man who was deeply worried about his mother. You may think I'm crazy, but I feel that you and I owe a great debt to Momma Smith, and though she and her boy are gone now, there remain millions of others like her in our nation.

Patriotism won't be found in the color of fireworks against an inky night sky. True patriotism is helping those who live in the inky dark night of poverty.

What are you doing for Momma Smith?

20

One Big Assumption

Advertisers typically assume that people are seeing and hearing their ads. Yet rarely is this the truth. In reality, the volume of advertising that gushes toward the mind is like a fire hose aimed at a teacup: there's simply too much coming at us to contain. Most of the information aimed at the brain is deflected, spilled, and lost. At the end of the day, precious little information is retained.

Will your advertising be part of that precious little, or is it being deflected, spilled, and lost?

The *Journal of Cognitive Neuroscience* is a publication read primarily by doctors and medical students who want to understand how human beings recognize and identify objects; use visual mental images; read, produce, and comprehend language; move and store new information in memory; and many other such things. (I think it makes sense for ad writers to read this stuff, too.)

A professor of psychology at Harvard, Stephen Kosslyn, recently wrote an insightful chapter on auditory pattern activation and encoding and how these are essential elements in language skills. Kosslyn tells us, "A word is like a key. When a word unlocks the correct stored memories, it is meaningful."

It is my assertion that the carefully guided recall of a series of such stored memories is the secret of powerful advertising. Do the words of your ads cause the listener to imagine a series of personal experiences? (The experiences can be real or imagined. The important thing is that they be recalled from the mind in such a manner as to actively engage the listener in your ad.) To put it plainly, the

See ch. 53, "What Do You See?"

I refer to the participant in your ad as the "listener" even though the ad in question may be a print ad. When silently reading the written word, it has been established that readers actually "hear" the words in their minds.

listener must be a participant in your advertising. You must cause him to imagine himself taking precisely the action you so artfully describe.

See "associative memory," p. 23.

Nothing of worth or weight can be achieved with half a mind, with a faint heart, and with a lame endeavor.

Isaac Barrow

21

Wernicke and Broca

Visual images are processed in the brain's visual cortex, located at the base of the skull, just above your spine. Immediately above the visual cortex, at the back of the cranium, is the visual association area, where visual memories are stored. (Stay with me, this gets interesting.)

Sound is processed in the auditory cortex, right above your ear. The memory of sound is stored in the auditory association area, which occupies most of the sides of your head. It's here that words and sounds are stored.

Strategically located where auditory association meets visual association is Wernicke's area, the spot where objects are named. When you imagine a golden, four-legged, African animal with irregular brown spots and an extremely long neck, it's Wernicke that attaches the word "giraffe" to the image. When you think of a famous landmark in Paris, a graceful metal structure known throughout the world, it's Wernicke that whispers, "Eiffel Tower, stupid." Wernicke is the king of nouns.

Wernicke's Area

Named for Carl Wernicke, the German neuropathologist who first described it in 1874, Wernicke's area appears to be crucial for language comprehension. People who suffer from neurophysiological damage to this area (called Wernicke's aphasia or fluent aphasia) are unable to understand content words while listening, and unable to produce meaningful sentences; their speech has grammatical structure but no meaning.

Auditory and speech information is transported from the auditory area to Wernicke's area for evaluation of significance of content words, then to Broca's area for analysis of syntax. In speech production, content words are selected by neural systems in Wernicke's area, grammatical refinements are added by neural systems in Broca's area, and then the information is sent to the motor cortex, which sets up the muscle movements for speaking.

Reference: Gray, Peter. *Psychology.* New York: Worth Publishing, 1994.

A Layman's Guide to the Brain

Were you aware that sight and sound are not only received by separate organs, but are stored and processed in totally separate areas of the brain? Did you know that more of the brain is devoted to sound than to sight? Does it surprise you to learn that the portion of the human brain that stores the memory of sound (9) touches more areas of the brain than any other? Notice the relative size and placement of the auditory association area (9), the auditory cortex (8), Broca's area (11), and Wernicke's area (10) compared with those areas designated for the storage and processing of sight (1 & 2).

Left Hemisphere

1. Visual cortex: primary visual perception
2. Visual association area: complex processing of visual information
3. Sensory association area: processing of multisensorial information
4. Primary somatosensory cortex: pain, pressure, position, movement, and temperature
5. Primary motor cortex: initiation of voluntary movement
6. Motor association cortex: coordination of complex movements
7. Prefrontal cortex: planning, emotion, judgment
8. Auditory cortex: hearing
9. Auditory association area: complex processing of sound
10. Wernicke's area: comprehension of spoken language
11. Broca's area: speech production and articulation

At the other end of auditory association lies Broca's area, a powerful extension of auditory association into the motor association cortex. The motor association cortex is the center of all physical action and Broca's area the center of action words. Broca energetically generates verbs, enthusiastically constructs sentences, and anxiously anticipates what others are about to say.

The objective of advertising is to influence the prefrontal cortex — the seat of emotion, planning, and judgment, located just across the motor association cortex, right behind your forehead. And the shortest leap to it is from Broca's area.

Broca's Area

In 1861, French surgeon and anthropologist Paul Broca first identified the section of the brain, in the left hemisphere on the inferior border of the precentral gyrus, that is involved in speech production, specifically assessing syntax of words while listening, and comprehending structural complexity. People suffering from neurophysiological damage to Broca's area (called Broca's aphasia or nonfluent aphasia) are unable to understand and make grammatically complex sentences. Speech will consist almost entirely of content words.

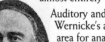

Auditory and speech information is transported from the auditory area to Wernicke's area for evaluation of significance of content words, then to Broca's area for analysis of syntax. In speech production, content words are selected by neural systems in Wernicke's area, grammatical refinements are added by neural systems in Broca's area, and then the information is sent to the motor cortex, which sets up the muscle movements for speaking.

Noticing that Broca's area was nearly always located in the brain's left hemisphere, which is the dominant hemisphere in a right-handed person, Paul Broca originally suggested that a person's handedness* would be opposite his Broca's area; thus, a left-handed person would have a right-hemispheric language specialization. However, most left-handers also seem to have left-hemispheric language specialization, too. Tricky business, eh? Researchers are still trying to figure it all out.

* "Handedness" is a vague term. Researchers define handedness based on different theoretical assumptions; some define it as the hand that performs faster or more precisely on manual tests; others say it is the hand that one prefers to use, regardless of performance. Some researchers argue that there are two types of handedness: (a) either left or right, and (b) either right or non-right. Others think there should be a third category to include ambidexterity. Still others argue that handedness should not be lumped into two or three or five categories but measured along the scale of a continuum.

Reference: Gray, Peter. *Psychology.* New York: Worth Publishing, 1994.

Vision and vision words happen at the back of the skull; action and action words happen at the front, in Broca's area, right next to the prefrontal cortex. The ear is right in the middle, the key to everything.

Describe what you want the listener to see, and she will see it. Cause her to imagine taking the action you'd like her to take, and you've brought her much closer to taking the action. The secret of persuasion lies in our skillful use of action words. The magic of advertising is in the verbs.

Just ask Broca.

Broca: The theater critic of the imagination; the part of the human mind that anticipates and ignores the predictable.

22

Second-Hand Knowledge

Which statement is stronger in a court of law, "I personally witnessed it, Your Honor," or "Someone told me, and he should know"?

So why, then, outside a courtroom, do we give the greater credence to second-hand knowledge?

Everything we know, or think we know, is the result of someone's observation — either a stranger's or our own. Why are we willing to trust a stranger's observations more than we trust our own? Why do we tend to swallow whole everything that is printed in a textbook? (Find a twenty-year-old science or technology textbook. Look at it closely and you'll see that much of what is printed there has since been proven wrong.)

Why do we place so much trust in second-hand knowledge? Have we become so adept at learning from others that we have forgotten how to think for ourselves?

I am fascinated by the number of people who will raise their hands and say to me with open hostility, "I was taught in college that we remember more of what we see than of what we hear, and that we remember best those things that we see *and* hear. So how do you explain all these theories of yours?" (Inwardly, this question always makes me sigh because the answer is so obvious that everyone should know it by now.)

Imagine a test using two focus groups. The first group hears ten words with a two-second interval between words. A second group is shown a screen with the same ten words printed on it. The screen remains visible for twenty seconds. The second group has a far higher retention of the words. Does this test prove the superiority of iconic memory? Does it really prove that we remember more of what we see than of what we hear?

No, it proves nothing of the sort.

The simple truth is that the human brain cannot understand the written word until it has been translated into the spoken word in the mind. Until the auditory association area of the brain "hears" a word, it has no meaning. Have you ever been reading in bed, then realized that your eyes have been scanning the same paragraph for several minutes, but you have absolutely no idea what it says? This is because your eyes are taking in words that are no longer being "heard" in your mind. The focus-group test proves only that retention increases with repetition. Those in group one heard the words only once. Given twenty seconds to stare at ten words, the second group "heard" the words an average of five times.

Echoic memory (also called echoic retention): The memory of things heard; sound information stored by the brain.

Iconic memory (also called iconic retention): The memory of things seen; visual data stored by the brain. More fragile and less reliable than echoic memory.

So now it's time for the follow-up challenge: "If, as you say, the ear is superior to the eye, then how do you explain speed reading?" Gosh. This is so obvious it's painful. Speed reading is possible because the rate of hearing greatly exceeds the rate of speaking, or even the speed of subvocalizing. There is a limit to the speed at which we can read, however, and it's precisely the speed of sound.

Any more questions?

The most fatal illusion is the settled point of view. Life is growth and motion; a fixed point of view kills anybody who has one.

Brooks Atkinson

23

Perceptual Reality

The room feels cold to one person, yet much too warm to another. So which of these is right? Is it possible for the same room to be at once too warm and too cold? Is there a universe that allows for the peaceful coexistence of such mutually exclusive truths?

The universe of matter and energy that surrounds us is utterly objective. The immutable laws of physics that govern space and time create a physical reality that is the same for us all.

Perceptual reality, however, is an entirely different matter.

When challenged with the question of the room's temperature, most people will answer, "It's a matter of opinion." But perceptual reality is much more than mere opinion. Perceptual reality is as real as a mother's love for her child; as real as encouragement, triumph, and joy.

When you're angry, is your anger real? Yet anger does not exist in physical reality. Does that mean it isn't there?

Physical reality is contained in the limited universe of matter and energy, while perceptual reality is uncontained in the boundless universe of the mind. Advertising doesn't affect physical reality in the slightest. It affects only the world of the mind. That's why the smallest minds smugly contend they are unaffected by advertising.

Small minds fear to make choices in the absence of verifiable facts, so they wrap themselves tightly in the security of physical reality and deny the existence of that which cannot be tested, proven, and measured. (Note: It is these same small minds that always shout loudest about the foolishness of faith in a world of science.)

So we have physical reality and perceptual reality, and of course there is spiritual reality as well.

But we'll leave that for another book.

24
A Problem with Details

James Cameron and Morgan Robertson never met, yet they have told us essentially the same story. Cameron's version is a major motion picture. Robertson's story is dead in the water.

What is it about Cameron's story that we like, and why do we reject the story of Robertson? In both stories, an "unsinkable" luxury liner on her maiden voyage, filled with wealthy and glamorous passengers, strikes an iceberg and sinks to the bottom of the North Atlantic. The catastrophe happens in April and there is a terrible shortage of lifeboats. In these elements, the stories are identical.

Is our problem with Robertson's version the fact that he doesn't pay enough attention to detail? Robertson tells us the ship is 800 feet long and displaces 70,000 tons of water. In Cameron's story, however, the numbers are correctly given as 882 feet and 66,000 tons. Another such error is the name of the ship: Robertson chooses to call her *Titan*. Cameron goes with the name *Titanic*.

See ch. 2, "Specifics and Generalities."

"But it wasn't the details that made us fall in love with James Cameron's story of *Titanic*," you protest. "Robertson probably just didn't write as good a love story as Cameron."

Although I agree with you, I'm still troubled by the details. You see, Morgan Robertson made these mistakes because he didn't wait for the *Titanic* to be built, designed, or even conceived before writing his story. Robertson published his book, *The Wreck of the Titan, or, Futility*, in 1898, fourteen years before *Titanic* ever left Southampton Harbor.

Morgan Robertson got the details wrong because he wrote about an historical event without waiting for the event to happen.

I sure hope he learned his lesson.

25

The Magic Square

reat photographers and graphic artists have long known of a peculiar spot on the canvas to which the eye is irresistably drawn. In any piece of two-dimensional art, this "magic square" is centered at the intersection of the upper and right matrix lines when a tic-tac-toe grid is drawn upon the face of the art.

Knowing that the eye will go the magic square, great artists always put something there for the eye to find. (This is not to be considered an unbreakable rule, only an interesting little tip for those times when you're needing focus on a graphics project.)

Consider the following examples:

Newspaper illustration
from the Spanish-
American War

Painting by
Leonardo da Vinci

Travel poster from the
Edwardian era

26

Huebner's Fifth Rule of Mountaineering: Never Look Where You Don't Want to Go

Like your customers, you can do only those things you have already "seen" yourself doing in your mind. You can do only what you have first imagined; when you imagine nothing, then nothing is exactly what you will create. What do you imagine for your future?

Preston Bradley tells us, "The world has a way of giving you what is demanded of it. If you are frightened and look for failure and poverty, you will get them, no matter how hard you may try to succeed. Lack of faith in yourself, in what life will do for you, cuts you off from the good things of the world. Expect victory and you make victory. Nowhere is this truer than in business life."

Tomorrow's reality is created by today's imagination. In a letter to his friends in the city of Philipi nearly 2,000 years ago, Paul writes, "Whatever is true, whatever is honorable, whatever is just, whatever is pure, whatever is lovely, whatever is gracious, if there is any excellence, if there is anything worthy of praise, think on these things."

It was good advice then, and it's good advice today.

Huebner's Six Rules of Mountaineering: See pp. 37–38.

Guard the secret theater of your heart. See nothing there that you do not want to see happen in reality.

Skill and confidence are an unconquered army.

George Herbert

27

Escape the Dungeon of Depression

A s the lack of sleep wore me down, a sense of hopelessness enveloped me. I knew that nothing I did could change the situation. There was nothing I could do. I was convinced that I was laboring under some kind of curse so that any efforts of my own to fight this situation were foredoomed to failure." — Percy Knauth

"I am now experiencing myself all the things that as a third party I have witnessed going on in my patients — days when I slink about depressed." — Sigmund Freud

"I have made a captive of myself and put me into a dungeon, and now I cannot find the key to let myself out." — Nathaniel Hawthorne

"I am now the most miserable man living. If what I feel were equally distributed to the whole human family, there would be not one cheerful face on earth. Whether I shall ever be better, I cannot tell. I awfully forebode I shall not. To remain as I am is impossible. I must die or be better it appears to me." — Abraham Lincoln

Have you ever been depressed? In your depression, did you say to those around you, "I can't help it, it's just how I feel"? According to the most recent medical journals, one person in five suffers from depression, and one in twenty suffers from a depression severe enough to require medical treatment. Depression in its various forms (insomnia, fatigue, anxiety, and so forth) is the most common complaint heard in doctors' offices today. Is there anything we can do about it? I believe there is.

Feelings follow actions. When we spend our time thinking about how we feel, we grow increasingly depressed. But when we spend our energies trying to make others feel better, we become increasingly satisfied and happy with our lives. You want a sure-fire cure for the blues? By an act of your will, find a person who needs help. Focus your mind on helping that person, even though you may not feel like it. Encourage him, even though you may desperately need encouragement yourself. As you become increasingly concerned about the other person, you will become less concerned about yourself, and the fog of depression will lift. In the words of Phil Johnson, "When you do not love a person, do what you would do if you did love him. Use the strength of your will to take actions that you do not feel. Your feelings will change soon enough."

Depression is insidious because it causes us to become fixated on how we feel, and the resulting self-absorption leads to even greater depression. Go back to the quotes at the beginning of this memo and count how often the speakers refer to themselves; the words "I," "me," "myself," and "my" occur twenty-seven times in four short statements. The person who asks, "How am I feeling right now?" is plummeting headfirst into a case of the blues just as certainly as if he had injected it into his arm with a needle. Most people believe they do what they do because of how they feel. In reality, the opposite is true: they feel what they feel because of what they do.

Now what are you going to do?

There is a more severe clinical form of depression that is caused by a chemical imbalance in the body. I do not pretend that my cure will work for this kind of depression.

Too many people overvalue what they are not and undervalue what they are.

Malcolm Forbes

28

Emily Lives Inside Herself

orn into a wealthy family in 1830, Emily has her photograph taken at the age of eighteen, then lives a remarkably uneventful life until she quietly passes at the age of fifty-five. It will be the only photograph ever made of her.

Incredibly shy, Emily asks her friends to speak to her through an open door from an adjoining room while she stands behind the wall. Her life consists of tending her garden and baking. She never travels, never marries, and rarely leaves her home. Emily lives in a world of imagination where words are all she requires to generate a series of vivid associations. She believes that words have the power to alter us irrevocably. I believe that she is right.

Though she is widely considered to be one of the greatest wordsmiths who ever lived, not even her own family knew that Emily Dickinson was a writer. It was only after her death that more than 1,700 of her poems were found hidden in a bureau drawer. Describing the power of words to envelop and devastate the listener, Emily wrote, "If I feel physically as if the top of my head were taken off, I know that is poetry."

Having had virtually no communication with the world, how could Emily Dickinson so richly describe the human experience? I believe the answer lies partly in physiology. We see, hear, feel, taste, and smell our environment with 100 million sensory receptors, but — because of our 10,000 billion synapses, with which we think and ponder and imagine — we are approximately 100,000 times more capable of experience in the invisible world of the mind than in the physical world that surrounds us.

Emily knew words to be the most powerful force there has ever been. Had she been inclined to start an advertising firm, it would

See ch. 18, "Living with Tarzan in the Jungle."

likely have become the most successful one in history. I believe Emily was sending a message to ad writers when she wrote

It is the Imagination
that lights
the Slow Fuse
of the Possible.

Imagination lights the fuse of the Possible with the magical fire of words. Have you ever seen the world of the Possible under the illumination of words? There are 100,000 places to go in the world of the Possible, with each one as richly textured as the world you currently see, hear, feel, taste, and smell.

Bringing things home from the world of the Possible to the land of Present Reality requires only that you build a bridge of words strong enough to carry your dream. Some people call this bridge Advertising. Some people call it Selling. Some call it Simple Persuasion.

Call it what you will, it is a bridge built of magical fire.

There is no frigate like a book
to take us lands away.

Emily Dickinson

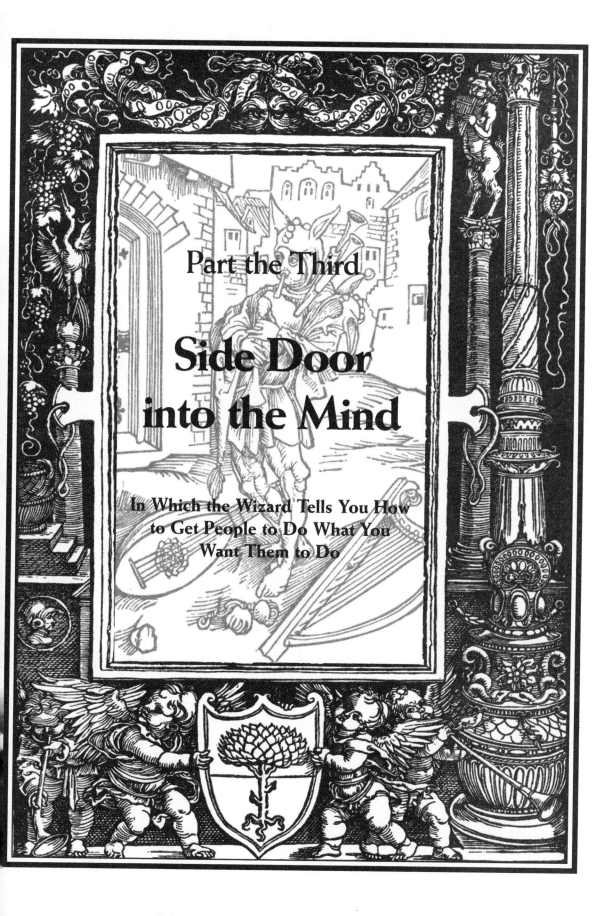

Part the Third

Side Door into the Mind

In Which the Wizard Tells You How
to Get People to Do What You
Want Them to Do

29

Sing a Little Song,
Dance a Little Dance

I am scheduled to speak at a luncheon of the American Marketing Association, a highly prestigious professional organization. As I turn into the parking lot of the swank country club where the meeting is to be held, I gaze across an endless sea of new luxury cars and think, "Maybe blue jeans and a turtleneck weren't the best way to dress after all." Walking into the ballroom, I see that my parking-lot premonition was right. These people give new meaning to the words "conservative business attire."

About twenty minutes into my talk, I hold out a copy of *The Wizard of Ads*. "This is my new book," I say, "and it's different from all the other books on advertising that you've ever read. It's hilariously funny in some parts and heartbreakingly sad in other parts, and it's for sale at the back of the room." Raising the book over my head, I lean into the microphone and whisper, "You'll laugh; you'll cry; you'll kiss seventeen bucks good-bye." Now I step out from behind the podium and begin to shout like the vamp at a James Brown concert, "Put your hands together and help me now! I'll laugh! (Clap) I'll cry! (Clap) I'll kiss seventeen bucks good-bye! (Clap) I'll laugh! (Clap) I'll cry! (Clap) I'll kiss seventeen bucks good-bye! (Clap)" I keep this up until most of the crowd is clapping and chanting with me, then step back behind the podium and finish my talk. Afterwards, I sell a record number of books.

My next speaking engagement is to a large group of professional freelance writers, mostly women. If the first bunch looked like Republican bank presidents, then this is a group of Cub Scout den mothers. There's even a table at the back of the room with chocolate chip cookies and milk. This time, I hold up the book and say, "This is a marvelous book. It will make you rich. It will make you thin. You'll be thin and rich. You'll be rich and thin." I then improvise a few little dance steps, throwing in all my best Elvis moves. The ladies clap and laugh until tears are dripping off their chins. At the end of the talk, they buy even more books than the bank presidents.

I'm not really a showman at heart, but I could think of no other way to test my theories:

Theory 1. Surprise is the foundation of delight and the beginning of persuasion. By surprising the audience, each of my little excursions into the absurd resulted in the sale of more books than would normally have been sold.

Theory 2. People tend to follow through with what they have heard themselves say they would do. Causing self-respecting businessmen to hear themselves say "I'll kiss seventeen bucks good-bye" resulted in the sale of more books.

Mental image: See ch. 30, "Surprising Broca."

Theory 3. When you are speaking to a deeply felt need — "It will make you thin" — it doesn't matter that the customer knows you can't possibly deliver what you have promised. The image of themselves as thin was successfully implanted into the ladies' minds, and that image was associated with the purchase of my book. Emotion beats intellect every time.

Am I a manipulative little sneak? I prefer to think of myself as a researcher. It's purely coincidental that I've decided to learn a few more dance moves.

The art of using moderate abilities to advantage often brings greater results than actual brilliance.

François de La Rochefoucauld

30

Surprising Broca

When Americans are in a funk, we say we've "got the blues." An Israeli will say she is "meduchdach," while an Italian will be "scoraggiato." A Japanese person calls this feeling "yuutsu," while a German will say he is "niedergeschlagen." The American expression, "the blues," is the only phrase that refers to a color, yet each of these people is attempting to describe exactly the same feeling. The mental image of boredom and mild depression is the same for each of them; they have simply attached different words to it. Neurologists tell me that such wordless mental images are the universal language of all humankind.

But if the whole human family thinks in the same language, then why do we speak in so many different ones?

According to cognitive neuroscience, our thoughts are composed of neither words nor pictures. Human thought is a speed-of-light progression of mental images, each one a complex composite of sound, shape, texture, color, smell, taste, and mood. Different languages are created only when different words are attached to these mental images in Wernicke's area of the brain.

Once a word has been attached to each mental image, the whole verbal jigsaw puzzle moves to Broca's area, where the selected words are arranged into understandable sentences. Only after the puzzle is assembled in Broca's area are we finally able to "speak our mind."

When Wernicke attaches the "usual" words and Broca arranges them in the "usual" order, the result can be painfully predictable: "Merlot is more full-bodied than Cabernet." But a little extra effort by Wernicke and Broca changes this boring sentence into an electric one: "Cabernet tastes of sunshine and rainbows, while Merlot is foggy, dark, and Gothic." Now everyone at the table is scrambling to have a taste.

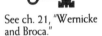

See ch. 21, "Wernicke and Broca."

Mental image: A complex composite of fragmented memories of sight, sound, texture, color, smell, taste, opinion, and mood. Contrary to popular belief, we think in neither words nor pictures, but with mental images.

Although none of the neurologists I've consulted can positively confirm or deny it, I am convinced that while a *speaker* uses Broca's area to arrange his words into understandable sentences, the *listener* uses Broca to anticipate and discount the predictable. When your listener hears only what she has heard before, it's difficult to keep her attention.

When speaking or writing, visualize Broca's area as a theater stage upon which your play will be performed in the listener's mind, and think of Broca as a theater critic — the judge who will determine whether or not to walk out on your play. If you will present your play on this mental stage and gain the smiling approval of the judge, you must electrify Broca with the thrill of the unexpected. "More full bodied" just won't do.

Such language causes Broca to be "niedergeschlagen."

Schema: The personal template, composed of personal experiences, suspicions, and superstitions, through which one views the world. A person's schema determines what Broca anticipates. For example, when the first seven notes of a musical scale are played, most people anxiously anticipate the eighth note. Should the eighth note not be played, the schema remains unsatisfied and Broca is surprised.

Engage the imagination by surprising Broca. Heighten anticipation by failing to satisfy your listener's schema.

31

The Ad Writer as Poet

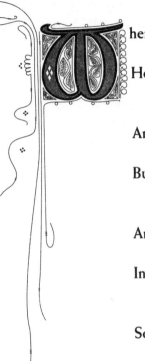

henever Richard Cory went downtown,
We people on the pavement looked at him:
He was a gentleman from sole to crown,
Clean favored, and imperially slim.

And he was always quietly arrayed,
And he was always human when he talked;
But still he fluttered pulses when he said,
"Good morning," and he glittered when he walked.

And he was rich — yes, richer than a king,
And admirably schooled in every grace:
In short, we thought that he was everything
To make us wish that we were in his place.

So on we worked, and waited for the light,
And went without the meat, and cursed the bread,
And Richard Cory, one calm summer night,
Went home and put a bullet through his head.

"Richard Cory," by Edwin Arlington Robinson (1869–1935)

See ch. 21, "Wernicke and Broca."

Finishing Robinson's emotional poem, our minds are flooded with remembered truths: "You can't judge a book by its cover." "Money can't buy happiness." "The mass of men live lives of quiet desperation." Certainly Robinson surprises Broca with the ending of "Richard Cory," but it is his skillful use of unpredictable words in unusual combinations throughout the poem that brings electricity to his writing.

Throughout the poem, Robinson invents new phrases that we instantly understand. When Robinson says, "We people on the pavement," we know exactly who he means, though we have never before heard the phrase. Two simple words, "imperially slim," cause us to see a vision of grand aristocracy: a handsome man with an elegant, regal bearing.

Every ounce a poet, Robinson resists the temptation to say that Richard Cory "made hearts skip a beat." (Such a phrase would have caused Broca to close his eyes and yawn.) "But still he fluttered pulses when he said, 'Good morning,' and he glittered when he walked."

Robinson startles Broca with a series of mental images that he sends tumbling toward the mind like boulders down a mountainside; we have barely dealt with the last one when another is upon us. A great poet gives the imagination no time to wander.

See "mental image," p. 70.

I am not suggesting that you write ads that rhyme. Such a thing would probably seem tedious and contrived. I am suggesting only that you saturate your mind with poetry. Listen to it and absorb it as though you were trying to learn a foreign language.

Go to the bookstore and buy a book of poetry, or go to the library and borrow one. Begin with Robert Frost, Carl Sandburg, and Emily Dickinson, then let your own taste take you where it will. Learn to unleash the power of words.

In your ads, use unpredictable words in unusual combinations. Surprise Broca. Don't satisfy the expectations of the schema.

S'habiller

32

A Spoonful of Sugar

The cozy melody rises to greet you like a familiar friend, and its lazy, carefree meandering takes you away to a quiet place, reminding you of the warmth of a peaceful afternoon in the Tom Sawyer summer of your childhood. You are listening to the theme song from *M.A.S.H.*

Were you aware that the melody has lyrics? I discovered this bit of trivia as a result of wandering through a video rental store without a specific title in mind. Scanning the shelves for movies I had not yet seen, I suddenly realized that everyone in America saw *M.A.S.H.* in 1970 except me. I rented the movie.

Much like the TV series that followed, Robert Altman's film opens with a helicopter scene and that amazingly innocuous Johnny Mandel theme song. The subtle difference is that in the movie, a vocalist croons a message of suicide with the bright-eyed innocence of a child.

The movie is forgettable, but the melody of that theme song is so utterly seductive ("Through early morning fog I see . . .") that I have breezily sung of suicide ("visions of the things to be . . .") for the past three weeks ("the pains that are withheld for me . . ."), never once realizing ("I realize and I can see . . .") that I was sipping psychological hemlock ("that suicide is painless . . ."). Such is the power of music .

"So I guess you're saying that it's good to use jingles in our broadcast ads?" Let me answer plainly: there is nothing better than a good musical jingle, and nothing worse than one that is average.

Unfortunately, most jingles are average.

But if music has the power of echoic intrusiveness to enter an unwilling mind and the tenacity of echoic retention to remain, then shouldn't we use it in all the ads we create? In theory, the answer is

Forgettable? Though a perceptive critic, perhaps ye Wizard doth sometimes err.
— Anonymous Student
JM

yes, but to say that all music is memorable is as silly as saying that all speeches are memorable. Just as it takes an unusual combination of words to engage the listener's imagination, it requires an unusual combination of notes and rhythm to surprise and enchant the mind. A powerful tool, music is the language of the soul in the hands of a master, but counterproductive in the hands of anyone else.

See ch. 21, "Wernicke and Broca."

You know at least a dozen writers of dazzling words, but do you know many masters of melody? It is far easier to master the language of men than to sing in the language of angels. 𝔛

Echoic intrusiveness: The tendency of unusual combinations of spoken* words, notes, or rhythms to lodge themselves in the listener's memory and play over and over in the mind.

*"Spoken" can mean "heard in the mind" (see "echoic memory," p. 55).

33

Way Too Stupid

A Frenchman lies on his back in a field and chews on a straw while staring at the clouds overhead and says, "Anything that is too stupid to be spoken is sung."

"Someone left the cake out in the rain. I don't think that I can take it, 'cause it took so long to bake it, and I'll never have that recipe again. Oh, noooo!"* "You're so vain I'll bet you think this song is about you. Don't you? Don't you? Don't you?"** "Ventura Highway in the sunshine, where the days are longer, the nights are stronger than moonshine."***

Would it surprise you to learn that our Frenchman made his observation just a few years after the Pilgrims landed at Plymouth Rock? Radio would not be invented for another two centuries. Was Voltaire having a vision of the future, or was he merely commenting on the phenomenon we have come to know as echoic retention?

"TwoAllBeefPattiesSpecialSauceLettuceCheesePicklesOnions OnaSesameSeedBun"?

Echoic retention causes people to remember things they never committed to memory, and a working knowledge of it gives one the ability to work miracles through the power of words. Echoic retention and the power of words are the heart and soul of advertising, though very few ad professionals understand it.

To infuse an ad with the power to persuade your customers, you must do one or more of the following:

1. Remind customers of what they already believe to be true, then associate your message to this "known" truth, thereby causing them to feel differently toward your product. (This is the definition of an emotional ad. This process is currently being labeled "branding" by people who are only now discovering its power.)

*"MacArthur Park," Jimmy Webb, 1968

**"You're So Vain," Carly Simon, 1972

***"Ventura Highway," Dewey Bunnell, 197[?]

See ch. 36, "Intellect vs. Emotion."

2. Ask customers to make a new decision based on new information that you have presented and substantiated in your ad. (This is an intellectual ad, the most common type in America, though few companies ever bother to substantiate their claims.)

3. Use unusual word combinations, rhythms, and melodies to sneak past the intellectual guard at the gate of the customer's mind. (This is an echoic ad. It can be intellectual, but more often it's emotional.)

See ch. 31, "The Ad Writer as Poet"; "echoic memory," p. 55.

No, I'm not talking about musical jingles. I'm talking about using unusual words in unpredictable combinations. I'm talking about the use of modified timing, inflection, pace, and tone in the ads you record for broadcast. The human voice is irresistible to the mind when used in a manner unexpected. This is true whether a reader is hearing his own voice in the quiet of his mind or whether he's hearing your voice through television or radio. It is predictability that turns the raging bull of language into the docile steer of dull advertising.

Are you emasculating your ads by using predictable phrases, styles, pace, or tone? Or are you using unexpected words as music to the mind?

34

Songs with Words, Pictures with People

In recent weeks, I've begun each of my seminars by asking an impromptu question of the audience: "Whose corporate image do you prefer? Häagen-Dazs or Ben and Jerry's?" Raising my hand as high as I can extend it, I continue: "All those who prefer the image of Häagen-Dazs, raise your hand." For the next several moments, my hand is the only one raised. "Now those who prefer the image of Ben and Jerry's . . . " Every hand in the room goes up in a single motion.

In 1978, childhood buddies Ben Cohen and Jerry Greenfield scraped together $12,000 to launch an ice cream shop from an abandoned gas station in Vermont. Today, Ben and Jerry are household heroes.

Was it the ice cream or was it the advertising?

The story of Häagen-Dazs begins with an eight-year-old boy who comes to America with his widowed mother in 1921. To support themselves, young Reuben and his mom squeeze lemons into test tubes to make refreshing lemon popsicles, which Reuben then sells to a grateful public on the streets of the Bronx. At age nineteen, Reuben launches Senator Frozen Products, and at forty-eight he creates Häagen-Dazs, a product that has taken him forty years to perfect.

Häagen-Dazs has a fabulous story to tell. So why aren't they telling it?

I believe Ben and Jerry's ice cream is more appealing than Häagen-Dazs only because it includes two special ingredients: (1) Ben and (2) Jerry.

Songs with words are recalled more quickly (and with greater accuracy) than music that has no words. Likewise, pictures with people in them are viewed more often (and longer) than pictures that have no people.

In your advertising, never forget: Words are electric and people are magnetic; people attract people.

Every ad is a story about someone or something. Who or what will be the subject of your story? Will your ads be about the product, the store, the owner, or the customer? Great ads are about the customer.

Average writers position the listener as an uninvolved bystander.

Good writers position the listener as an interested observer.

Great writers involve the listener as an active participant.

Speak to the felt need of the listener and make him a participant in your ad by using the word "you."

Nothing draws a crowd like a crowd.

P. T. Barnum

35

John Young's Fortune

Light is fading and snow is falling, a reflective white coat to warm a surreal, half-lit world. The scene indoors is even more surreal as a man in a blue work shirt with the name "Fred" on the pocket gives John Young the opportunity of a lifetime. "John, you've got to help me sell air-conditioning systems in February and March, or I won't be able to hang on until summer."

Like most HVAC contractors, Fred makes money during the heat of the summer, then spends it to survive the cold winter. Last year's mild summer meant fewer air conditioners sold, so now Fred's company is on its financial knees. "Can you help me sell air conditioners in February, John? Will you help me save my company?"

Most marketing consultants would have searched for a mailing list of homeowners with broken air conditioners, but John Young is of that rare breed whose faith lies not in scientifically targeted direct-mail lists but in the power of words. On February 5th, John mails a three-page letter to 5,000 randomly selected homes. The envelope contains no fancy brochure — just 1,041 carefully chosen words written in a casual style.

During the next seven weeks, Fred's company sells more air conditioners than it has ever sold before, breaking the sales record of even the hottest and most profitable summer. Fred's installation crews are working overtime and on weekends. "John," says Fred, "I think you're onto something."

Two years later, John Young and his partner Jim Abrams build a national member organization wherein John performs his wizardry in marketing and Jim teaches members to be Wizards of Finance. John's letter helps members sell nearly $500 million worth of air-conditioning systems; it's the first of many things they do to help their members grow their companies. A few years later, Jim and John take a spin-off of their organization to Wall Street, where it becomes one of the most successful IPOs of that year, netting them more than $20 million apiece.

Service Experts is currently traded on the New York Stock Exchange under the symbol SVE

What does John Young tell Fred's customers? He simply points out that people who wait until summer to discover they need a new air conditioner are usually forced to endure several days of waiting in the heat as overworked installation crews scramble to meet the need; that buying an air conditioner in the wintertime means you'll get a better price, greater product choice, and more careful installation. In other words, he appeals to the customer's intellect with simple, straightforward truth.

Unlike most great writers, John Young doesn't really like to write, but he definitely knows the value of words. Apologizing to his long-time partner, John says, "Jim, if I had known we were going to be paid $40,000 a word, I swear I'd have written a longer letter."

A smart businessperson is one who makes a mistake, learns from it, and never makes it again. A wise businessperson is one who finds a smart businessperson and learns from him how to avoid the mistakes he made.

Jim Abrams

36

The Six Tugs-of-War:
1. Intellect vs. Emotion

It's 1975. I'm watching the hit movie *Jaws* from the back row. The scene on the screen is quiet and calm, without even a hint of trouble on the horizon. The actors are engaged in inconsequential dialogue on a boat floating lazily under sunny skies. It's time to go for popcorn.

As I'm about to step from the darkness of the theater into the bright lights of the lobby beyond, I hear a collective, strangled gasp and look behind me to see 400 people floating above their seats in a series of spastic positions worthy of *Seinfeld*'s Kramer. It seems the shark has unexpectedly leaped into the back of the boat, utterly terrifying everyone watching. A moment later, as 400 posteriors land in 400 padded seats, I realize that everyone watching was emotionally in that boat when the shark leaped out of the water.

Wait a minute. Intellectually, these people know they're not in the water. Intellectually, they know it's only a movie. Intellectually, they know it's a mechanical shark! If I'm a character in a cartoon drawing, this is the moment when the little light bulb appears over my head: Intellect and emotion are not connected! Consequently, ad

Ads must appeal to either the intellect or the emotions. An intellectual ad leads us to a new decision based on new information. An emotional ad tells us only what we've always known, but causes us to feel different about it. Tom Bodette reminded us of what we already knew, that "Motel 6 has the lowest prices of any national chain," but Tom made us feel different about it. He replaced our mental image of "cheap and tacky" with one of "clean and simple." The straightforward and unpretentious charm of his statement, "We'll leave the light on for ya," caused us to question the real value of chocolate mints on our pillows and tiny bottles of avocado body balm in our shower stalls. The ad campaign for Motel 6 was a brilliant emotional campaign.

writers must choose whether to speak to the customer's intellect or to her emotions.

In the years since my epiphany, I've realized that good intellectual ads suggest to the customer that she make a new decision based on new information, then substantiate the ad's claims with indisputable evidence. But rarely are even the best intellectual ads as productive as those that engage our emotions. (Is there a time when an advertiser should speak to the intellect? Absolutely! It's just doesn't come as often as most advertisers believe.)

An emotional ad is one that reminds the customer of something she's always known or has long suspected. Emotional ads build on the foundation of the customer's own experience while subtly inserting a new perspective. As a result of this newfound perspective, the customer will have new feelings attached to the product or service featured in the ad. Psychologists call this "associative memory."

The simple truth is that we usually do what feels right, then use intellectual logic to justify what our emotions have decided. Then we tell ourselves that we've made "the intelligent decision." Does anyone besides me think this is funny?

Do your ads speak to the customer's mind or to her heart? Will you more likely win her with intellect or with emotion? This is the question that must be answered before your ad writer ever sets pen to paper.

Have you answered it?

See "associative memory," p. 23.

To win the confidence of the listener, agree with her schema (see p. 71). Tell the listener she's "been right all along."

Words are electric; they should be chosen for the emotional voltage they carry. (See the brain map on page 51. Note the proximity of Broca's area to the section of the brain that controls emotion and judgment.)

Logic rarely prevails in arguments of the heart.

A man convinced against his will is unconvinced still.

Pastor Phil Johnson

37

The Six Tugs-of-War:
2. Time vs. Money

If saving money were as important to us as most advertisers believe, there would be no such thing as convenience stores. We would cook more meals at home, and Federal Express would not exist.

The truth is that Americans have more money than any society in the history of the world, and what we are buying with that money is time. It has become the currency of our generation.

In 1985, the average American citizen spent about 10 hours per month in a shopping mall. Ten years later that number had dropped to only 3.5 hours. Though our spending in malls had not measurably declined, we were spending it in two-thirds less time. In just ten short years, comparison shopping had become a thing of the past.

"You and I are going less often, we're staying a shorter period of time, and we're visiting fewer stores while we're there, which is really three strikes," says Albany, New York–based retail consultant Jeff Corcoran in *American Demographics Magazine* (September 1996). "That's bad news for the malls."

The decade between 1985 and 1995 saw the emergence of the category killers — Toys "R" Us, Home Depot, Staples, Circuit City, and the like — a new breed of stores that gave us total confidence we were going to leave with whatever we had come to buy. On April 6, 1997, the *New York Times* reported, "Fully one-third of the retail dollars spent in 1996 were spent in a superstore that did not exist ten years ago."

See ch. 8, "Category Dominance."

Amazingly, category killers rarely deliver the lowest prices. What they deliver, instead, is a savings of time. We go to Toys "R" Us to buy Barbie's Summer Dream House because we don't want to spend all afternoon looking for it. We don't really care whether we pay the lowest possible price.

Today's shoppers are going directly to the store they feel is most likely to have what they want, and they are walking in the front door with every intention of buying. Category killers don't just give the competition a run for its money, they eliminate it by design.

Which category do you kill? ✹

Time and money are interchangeable. You can always save one by spending more of the other.

Pennie Williams

38

The Six Tugs-of-War:
3. Opportunity vs. Security

I'm sitting at the conference table when a prospective client lays a large check in front of me. He covers the check with his hand and says, "If I give you this money, what will you guarantee me?" It's a question I'm asked routinely, so I lay my hand on top of his, look into his eyes, and give him my standard answer: "I guarantee that you'll never see this money again."

The only fool greater than the one who expects big results from small changes is the fool who believes big changes can be accomplished without risk. Opportunity and security are inversely proportionate: as one goes up, the other goes down. It's a fundamental law of the universe.

In his video *Paradigm Pioneers,* Joel Barker tells a story about two pivotal groups, the pioneers and the settlers, and the roles they played in America's westward expansion. As Joel tells it, the pioneers were the ones who charged off into an unknown wilderness and blazed new trails for the settlers who would later follow. The settlers, being somewhat risk averse, would sit and wait in the relative security of the towns along the frontier, occasionally sending a message down the trail asking, "Is it safe out there?" Finally, the response would arrive from the pioneers: "Yes, it's great! Come and join us." In today's business world, however, when the settlers ask the pioneers, "Have you proven the idea will work? Is it safe out there?" the pioneers are answering, "Yes, it's wonderful, but there's nothing left for you!"

Do you have the courage to be a pioneer, or will you live your life as a settler?

"If you are looking for perfect safety, you will do well to sit on a fence and watch the birds; but if you really wish to learn you must mount a machine and become acquainted with its tricks by actual trial." This is what Wilbur Wright, a bicycle mechanic, told the Western Society of Engineers on September 18, 1901. Since powered flight was considered impossible, the engineers laughed at him. This photo of Wilbur (at the controls) was taken two years and three months later.

Try a thing you haven't done three times. Once, to get over the fear of doing it. Twice, to learn how to do it. And a third time, to figure out whether you like it or not.

Virgil Thomson (advice given at age 93)

39

The Six Tugs-of-War:
4. Style vs. Substance

Shoes, fragrances, clothing, and soft drinks are often sold with ads that are "artsy" and "fluffy," and every time one of these campaigns becomes a big hit, some car manufacturer will begin an equally fluffy campaign to sell automobiles. Those campaigns invariably fail.

Products that are mostly style can be sold with ads that are mostly style. Products of substance, however, require ads of equal substance.

Is your product mostly style or mostly substance?

In 1994, Pennie and I flew to London, the home of DeBeers, to speak at the Centennial Anniversary Celebration of the Goldsmiths of the United Kingdom. We had been invited to speak there because several of America's most successful jewelers are clients of our firm, and the British were hoping we'd share our secrets with them. So we did.

Looking out over an ocean of highly intellectual jewelers from England, Ireland, Scotland, and Wales, I calmly informed them that no one really cared whether a diamond was the world's hardest substance. "Furthermore, it's usually a mistake to talk about your precious Four C's: Color, Cut, Clarity and Carat weight. When a person pays for a diamond," I said, "what he's really buying is the reaction of other people. The man pictures the reaction of the woman he loves; the woman imagines the reactions of her friends, co-workers, and neighbors." Pleasant smiles were turning into frowns all across the room as I concluded, "If you want to sell diamonds, don't waste your time describing the diamond itself. Describe the reaction of others."

You could've heard a pin drop. It was as though I had attacked their religion — and in a way I suppose I had. British jewelers deeply believe that the purchase of a diamond should be an intellectual transaction.

See ch. 36, "Intellect vs. Emotion."

That's why shockingly few diamonds are sold in England.

40

The Six Tugs-of-War:
5. Pain vs. Gain

Which would you rather have:

    1. a sure gain of $3,000, or

    2. an 80 percent chance of winning $4,000 and a 20 percent chance of winning nothing?

Now choose between

1. a sure loss of $3,000 and

2. an 80 percent chance of losing $4,000 and a 20 percent chance of losing nothing.

In their research on the process of human decision making, Daniel Kahneman and Amos Tversky clearly established that when the identical question is posed in slightly different ways, the resulting answers can be radically different.

Of particular note was their observation that "losses loom larger than gains" — specifically, that our willingness to accept risk is higher when we are facing possible loss than when the identical risk is presented in terms of potential gain.

In the first example, most people are unwilling to accept the risk. They opt for the "sure" $3,000, though pure mathematical probabilities make the second choice slightly more attractive (0.8 × $4,000 = $3,200). In the second example, however, more than 90 percent of those surveyed choose to accept the risk of losing an additional $1,000 to gain the 20 percent chance of losing nothing. Professors Kahneman and Tversky, at the University of Chicago, proved it again and again: the average person avoids risk when seeking gains, but is willing to embrace risk to avoid losses.

Sales trainers have long known this and often teach their students to phrase things in terms of potential loss. "You'd hate to return tomorrow and find that someone else had purchased this item, now, wouldn't you?" The pain-versus-gain theory is not so easily applied to advertising, however, because it presupposes that the subjects have been successfully reached with your message of potential loss — a very dangerous assumption in advertising.

See "mental image," p. 70; "first mental image," p. 117.

In reality, ads that speak to the fear of loss must necessarily conjure a negative first mental image, and in so doing, they will often alienate the listener. When confronted with an uncomfortable mental image, a percentage of the public instinctively opt not to "participate" with the ad; they direct their attention elsewhere. Moreover, those who casually participate with such ads often associate the negative mental image with the advertiser who presented it, and the campaign becomes counterproductive.

Although the fear of loss may be more powerful than the hope of gain, it's usually a mistake to use fear as a motivator in your ads. The first objective of every ad is to successfully engage the imagination of the listener with a thought more attractive than the one that currently occupies the listener's mind. How attractive are the mental images in your ads?

41

The Six Tugs-of-War:
6. Sight vs. Sound

ave you ever stopped to consider why Congress voted in 1970 to outlaw the use of sound to sell tobacco? No one in America has heard a radio or television ad for tobacco since January 1, 1971, yet most adults born before 1960 can still sing, "Winston tastes good, like a . . . " though not a single one of us ever intended to learn that melody.

It's interesting that the government waited nearly thirty years before placing even minimal restrictions on the visual advertising of tobacco. Tens of thousands of full-color magazine ads and full-page newspaper ads appeared in our publications. Hundreds of thousands of billboards were planted from coast to coast. Colorful signage was installed at sporting events, and every convenience store in America was plastered with tobacco posters and expensive point-of-purchase displays. But all these things combined were not enough to overcome the silence. Public opinion of tobacco products continued to erode year after year. Though visual advertising received billions of tobacco dollars each year, it was never able to compensate for the semi-hypnotic effects of sound. The tobacco companies learned that it's difficult to win our hearts when they are denied access to our ears. (The government is smarter than you realized, right?)

You hear even when you aren't listening. That's why you could always repeat what the teacher had just said every time she stopped and asked, "Are you listening?" even though you hadn't been listening. You hear even when you're fast asleep! (How else would you know when there's a prowler in the house?) Sound is intrusive, and the memory of sound is awesome.

Neurologists tell us that what comes through our ears stays in our minds for nearly five full seconds before it begins to fade. Conversely, whatever enters the eyes is gone in less than a second. This is why eyewitnesses can always agree on precisely what they heard, but none can recall with clarity quite what it was they saw. By the time eyewitnesses realize the importance of what they've seen, the critical second has usually passed and clear memory of the vision is gone.

See "echoic memory," "iconic memory," p. 55, "echoic intrusiveness," p. 75.

The greatest liar who ever lived was the one who first said, "One picture is worth a thousand words." Don't you believe it.

Echoic memory is trustworthy; iconic memory is not. "The ear long remembers what the eye soon forgets."

42

Are You Driving the Dog Crazy?

You already know that Pavlov used an echoic recall cue (the sound of a bell) to implant an associative memory into the mind of his dog. But have you ever wondered why Pavlov chose to use sound rather than sight? The answer is simple: because it's easier.

Dogs, like people, can close their eyes but they cannot close their ears. To implant an iconic recall cue, Pavlov would first have had to gain the visual attention of the dog. In addition, an iconic recall cue would have taken much longer to implant, due to the highly fragmented retention of visual memory in the brain.

In spite of these difficulties, Pavlov did, in fact teach a second dog to salivate by using the shape of a circle as an iconic recall cue. In this experiment, the dog was trained to salivate when shown the circle and to cease salivating when shown a long, narrow oval. Gradually, the shape of the oval was transformed so that it became more and more circular. When the difference between the circle and the oval was very slight, "the dog became highly agitated and the previously conditioned reflex was lost."

See "associative memory," "recall cue," p. 23.

Pavlov intentionally sent the dog mixed signals and described the result as "experimentally induced neurosis" in the dog. To put it plainly, the dog got extremely irritated and began to ignore Pavlov completely.

Today's buying public is not very different from that dog. To cause people to take the action you desire, your message must be focused and repetitive and speak to a need the customer feels. Mixed signals will only cause the public to ignore your ads completely.

Are you sending the public mixed signals in your ads? Are you guilty of irritating the dog? If so, you should consider a dramatic change in your ad campaign. Why not uncover the story that is uniquely and wonderfully your own? When the dog hears you sing your own beautiful song and finds that it's a song about him, I'll wager he'll be willing to do whatever you want him to do.

See ch. 11, "Digging for the Diamond."

Do you know what song to sing? Are you willing to sing it again and again?

The greatest mistake is to imagine that we never err.

Thomas Carlyle

43

How Long Is the Race?

ow tell me this: how long do you plan to be in business? Are you going for the hundred-meter dash, or would you like to be in the lead at the end of the marathon? Oh, really? Then why do you advertise as though this weekend were the last time your customers will ever have the opportunity to buy from you?

Short-term advertising — the sprint — is a race for fools. As a marketing strategy, it's self-defeating to train your customers to sit on the sidelines waiting for your next "Moonlight Madness Sale." You should be conditioning them to think of you automatically whenever they need what you're selling.

Here are the runners:

1. Newspaper is a sprinter, an information-delivery vehicle that reaches only those buyers who are in the market for the product *right now*. Though the advertiser pays to reach all readers, the only people who will see a newspaper ad are those who are looking specifically for what's being advertised. You'll see immediate results from your newspaper ads — but you'll have escaped the attention of those who are not consciously in the market for your product or service.

2. The Yellow Pages are like the weekend jogger, thudding along with no particular goal in mind. They're a service directory for shoppers who have no preference; when people don't know who to call, they pull out the Yellow Pages. As an advertiser, do you really want to take your chances as a face in the Yellow Pages crowd? The highest goal of advertising is to convince the customer of your worth long before he needs what you sell.

3. Sound — intrusive, irresistible sound — makes electronic media the long-distance runner of advertising. Broadcast wins the

hearts of customers *before* they're in the market for your product. If your goal is to be the first into the mind of your customer when he needs what you sell, and to be the company he feels the best about, you should invest in the intrusive nature of sound with the reliability of its echoic retention.

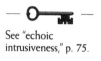

See "echoic intrusiveness," p. 75.

I'm always fascinated by people who say, "I tried advertising in electronic media, and it didn't work for me." Invariably, their tests were conducted according to rules that highly favored newspaper. They were looking for a quick payoff, and newspaper is definitely the best sprinter: you get what you get immediately, but it doesn't get better and better. Radio and television are marathon runners — the longer you continue, the better they work. They're a better investment in the long run than newspaper or Yellow Pages ads.

If you want to gamble on who's going to be in the lead at the end of thirty days, put your money on newspaper to win. But if your race is scheduled to run longer than six months, mortgage the house to buy TV and radio. It's only in the longer races that marathon runners show us what they've got.

When, Why, and How to Use Print Media

Direct mail: Justifiable when used for sending invitations to a private event, or for sending follow-up materials to a customer who has requested them.

Magazine: Trade magazines can be very effective when you need to reach a small number of people scattered across a large geographic area — for example, an ad in a banking trade magazine to sell software for running a bank. (Write the words first, then support the words with pictures — never the other way around.)

Outdoor: Imagine a black billboard with white letters: "We'll leave the lights on for ya." No logo, just the recall cue. When you have an echoic recall cue that is deeply established, outdoor advertising can be a very low-cost way to trigger the memory of your broadcast ads.

Newspaper: When you absolutely have to dump excess inventory or when you need to raise cash for an emergency but don't want to train your future customers to wait for your next sale, run a quarter- to half-page ad in the newspaper. Make the product, price, and time limit very large and bury the name of your company in small print at the bottom. Only those readers who are immediately in the market for your product will be reached.

44

The Midnight Street Sweeper

ow often have you heard a person say, "Let me sleep on it"? What is it that changes during the night that causes us to say, "Things always look better in the morning"? Why does sleep create such a difference in our outlook?

Sleep helps us cope with a world of too many sights, sounds, questions, problems, opportunities, emotions, and distractions. Sleep, the ever-faithful street sweeper of the mind, is what lets us keep our sanity in this overcommunicated world. Sleep: God's gift for purging the mind of the noise of the day.

It is only because of the cleansing effects of sleep that ads require relentless repetition. As odd as this may sound, the customer's retention of your advertising message will be determined largely by the ratio of ad repetition to customer sleep. The goal of a long-term (branding) campaign is to expose the listener to the identical ad approximately three times within each seven nights' sleep, fifty-two weeks a year. (In a short-term campaign, there's no such thing as too much repetition. Buy all the repetition that your budget will allow, and pray that it's enough.)

Establishing brand identity is like climbing a muddy mountain: three steps forward, two steps back, three steps forward, two steps back. You must have sufficient repetition (and patience) to overcome the cleansing effects of sleep.

On most radio stations, you can achieve a 3 frequency (meaning the identical listener will hear the ad three times) with nearly two-thirds of the station's weekly cume (total audience) with just twenty-one ads a week (plus or minus two ads) scheduled Monday through Sunday, 6 AM–7 PM (6 AM–8 PM if the late-evening news on television is at 11 PM instead of 10 PM). This odd little formula is due to the predictable

See "branding," p. 22.

See ch. 58, "Radio Scheduling."

patterns of listening that are unique to radio. Since viewer patterns on television are driven by viewer loyalty to specific shows rather than loyalty to specific TV stations, there is no comparable simple formula available for television or any other medium. Sorry.

When scheduling television ads, look for shows that air daily rather than weekly. You will reach fewer people as a result but will gain the priceless advantage of repetition. (See "critical equation," p. 129.)

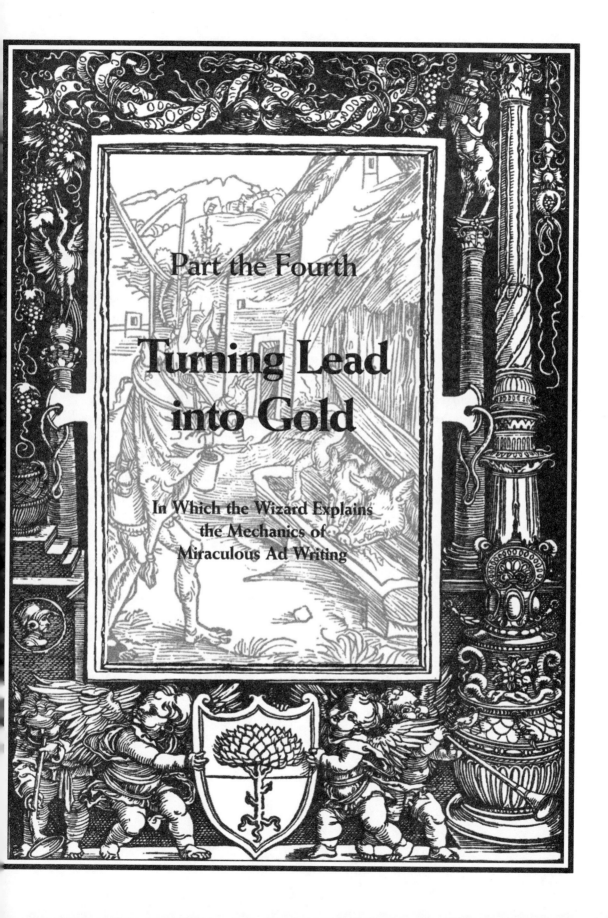

Part the Fourth

Turning Lead into Gold

In Which the Wizard Explains
the Mechanics of
Miraculous Ad Writing

45

Did Rembrandt Paint by Number?

The problem with being known as the "Wizard of Ads" is that people expect me to give them step-by-step formulas for successful advertising — as though winning the hearts of the public should be as easy as following the instructions on a paint-by-number kit. Since these people are looking for the kinds of answers one might find in a book for dummies, I did a little research. I learned that, among the 829 "Dummies" books currently on the market, there is no *Advertising for Dummies*.

You can get *Mutual Funds for Dummies, Law for Dummies, Business Plans for Dummies, Negotiating for Dummies, Time Management for Dummies,* and *Accounting for Dummies,* but you'll find no *Advertising for Dummies.* There's *Sales Prospecting for Dummies, Sales Closing for Dummies, Public Speaking for Dummies,* and *Shakespeare for Dummies;* but *Advertising for Dummies?* No way. As bizarre as this may sound, there's even *Beauty Secrets for Dummies, Dating for Dummies, Sex for Dummies, Pregnancy for Dummies, Parenting for Dummies,* and *Divorce for Dummies.* (No, I'm not exaggerating. There really are 829 different books for dummies.)

My research confirmed two things I had long suspected: (1) There are at least 829 things that are easier to explain than advertising. (2) People are quick to call themselves "dummies" when they want you to make difficult things easier to understand.

Your customer, however, is not a dummy. She is a warm, witty, intelligent woman whose response to contrived and predictable advertising will be much the same as her reaction to those detestable little pictures that come from painting by number. Great ad campaigns are never the result of a dummy following a formula. Great ad campaigns, like great paintings, are the result of talent meeting inspiration.

If you have the talent to create great ads, the key to your success will be to find someone who can inspire you. If you don't have the ability to create great ads, but your passion for your business gives you the ability to inspire the person whose talent lies in the power of words, find such a person and inspire him. I predict you'll enjoy great success together.

In the unfortunate event that you own a business for which you have no passion, let me offer you this heartfelt advice: Sell that business or close it, but definitely change careers. Your life is too precious to spend it doing something that leaves you empty inside.

If you insist on remaining in a business for which you have no passion, let me recommend two books: First, get a copy of *Coping with Depression*, by Sharon Carter and Lawrence Clayton ($6.95). Second, look for a book called *Bankruptcy for Dummies*. If it hasn't yet been written, I'm sure it will be soon. Bankruptcy is merely a series of simple steps that require neither talent nor passion. It's nothing at all like successful advertising.

When his ad writer is a poet,
the business owner will be a king.

The Wizard

46

Huebner's Second Rule of Mountaineering: No Guts, No Glory

The courageous respond instinctively to the law of the universe that rewards risk. Mountain climbers like Jim Huebner ponder this law as they stare across the dark chasm of possible catastrophe and say, "No guts, no glory." Likewise, the courageous businessperson stares across a similar chasm and says, "Nothing ventured, nothing gained."

Huebner's Six Rules of Mountaineering: See pp. 37–38.

The ancient Greek Thucydides may have been the first to comment on society's admiration of the courageous when he said, "They are sure to be esteemed bravest who, having the clearest sense of the pains and pleasures of life, do not on that account shrink from danger." But it was William DeMille who said it most charmingly: "I have always admired the ability to bite off more than one can chew and then chew it."

Yes, the world admires the courageous. Are you courageous? If so, be careful that you are not also idealistic and naïve. Your courage will not always bring you glory and reward; you will occasionally be called upon to pay failure's price. Only a fool risks what he is not prepared to lose.

Are you prepared to pay the price of failure, or are you just a tin soldier who has listened to one too many motivational tapes?

Tin soldiers are those who whine about their losses, beginning too many sentences with the words "If only." The truly courageous consider the price of failure merely a down payment on future success.

Who bravely dares must sometimes risk a fall.

Tobias George Smollett

47

Have You Calculated Your APE?

he APE is short, but very powerful. With long arms that reach into scheduling, copy writing, production, and reputation, it can predict with uncanny accuracy the success of any ad campaign. The "APE" is the *advertising performance equation*:

$$SoV \times IQ \times PEF \times MPo = Sales\ Volume$$

To better understand the APE, you must consider the three separate equations it combines:

Share of Voice (SoV) × Impact Quotient (IQ) = Share of Mind

Share of Mind × Personal Experience Factor (PEF) = Share of Market

Share of Market × Market Potential (MPo) = Sales Volume of the Advertiser

Exercise: Calculate the impact on share of market and annual sales volume for an advertiser with a PEF of 1.8 versus an advertiser with a PEF of 0.6. (Hint: The company scoring a 1.8 will get three times the results from its advertising.)

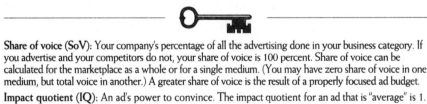

Share of voice (SoV): Your company's percentage of all the advertising done in your business category. If you advertise and your competitors do not, your share of voice is 100 percent. Share of voice can be calculated for the marketplace as a whole or for a single medium. (You may have zero share of voice in one medium, but total voice in another.) A greater share of voice is the result of a properly focused ad budget.

Impact quotient (IQ): An ad's power to convince. The impact quotient for an ad that is "average" is 1.

Share of mind: Share of voice that has been adjusted in the customer's mind by the impact quotient of the ad. It's possible to have a smaller share of voice due to spending less money than your competitors, yet still have a greater share of mind as the result of ads with a higher impact quotient.

Personal experience factor (PEF): A customer's experience with your company. Your PEF is, effectively, your reputation. Perfect neutrality scores a PEF of 1. The growth or decline of a business will usually follow that company's PEF as it rises and falls above and below a score of 1. Your PEF score cannot be changed through advertising. (See ch. 64, "The World Inside Your Door.")

Share of market: Your percentage of business in your business category.

Market potential (MPo): The total dollars available in a business category.

The details of how to calculate an IQ score for an ad and a PEF score for an advertiser were unavailable, though I understand the process is taught at the Wizard's Academy.
— Ray Bard, Publisher

48

"All for One, and One for All"

Though few people have ever realized it, successful advertising requires a triad as closely knit as the legendary Three Musketeers of Alexandre Dumas.

Share of voice (SoV) is in the hands of the advertising sales representative. It's the sales rep's job to deliver the greatest share of voice the business owner's budget will allow. Beyond this, the rep can do very little.

Impact quotient (IQ) is the responsibility of the ad writer, the member of the team who is most often overlooked and underpaid. Without persuasive ads, share of voice is of little benefit, yet you'll often find the ad writer at the very bottom of the food chain. How well do you know the person who's creating your ads? More important, how well does he know you?

Personal experience factor (PEF) is entirely the business owner's turf. Good advertising cannot be expected to erase the customer's memory of a disappointing experience or reverse the impact of a bad reputation. Conversely, the positive momentum generated by good advertising will be accelerated by a customer's happy experience. Is your company careful to deliver all that your ads promise?

For the past thirty years, demographic targeting, gross rating points, and media mix have fostered an atmosphere of finger pointing and blame shifting within the advertising community. Utterly ignoring these sacred cows, the APE (advertising performance equation) reconciles the divergent responsibilities of the sales rep, the ad writer, and the business owner.

See ch. 64, "The World Inside Your Door."

See ch. 47, "Have You Calculated Your APE?"

Legendary ad campaigns are born in that magical instant when each member of this unlikely trio realizes that success is impossible without the best efforts of the other two. "All for One, and One for All."

Media dominance: The position owned by the advertiser with the greatest share of voice.

Never make the mistake of doing two things halfheartedly when you can do one thing wholeheartedly. Always dominate a medium.

If you cannot dominate all of radio, dominate a single station. If you cannot dominate a whole station, dominate a single daypart on that station. If you cannot dominate all of television, then dominate a single hour of the day. If you cannot dominate an hour, dominate a single TV show or cable channel. Then, when your business has grown, dominate a second and a third.

Never say, "We've already reached these people, now we need to reach some new ones." Advertising is obliterated by sleep, the great eraser of the mind (see "critical equation," p. 129). Consequently, people don't stay "reached" any more than a lawn stays mowed. The key to media dominance is relentless repetition.

Though an enemy might prevail against one who is alone, two will withstand him, and a cord of three strands is not quickly broken.

Solomon

49

You Can't Hear a Decimal Point

A full-size, long-stemmed American Beauty rose in twenty-four-karat pure gold. Measuring more than fourteen inches from the tips of its delicate petals to the bottom of its substantial stem, this gold rose is fantastically special. Utterly unique. One of a kind. Just like she is. At twenty-nine-ninety-nine, it's the solitary rose she will cherish forever; a rose that will have the neighbors talking for years to come. Available exclusively at _____ Jewelers."

Sounds great, doesn't it? So tell me, is the rose thirty dollars or three thousand?

Translating a print ad into a radio ad is a lot like translating English into Japanese. It should never be done word for word.

Prices ending in "ninety-nine" are prices written for the eye. The ear works a whole other way.

One of our clients objected when we rounded the prices on a list of items for a radio ad. Three-ninety-nine became four dollars; four-ninety-nine became five hundred dollars; and ninety-nine-ninety-nine became ten thousand dollars. The client wanted "accuracy" and demanded that we change the prices back to the series of ninety-nines. The resulting radio ad sounded like an auctioneer gone berserk. Accuracy was not accomplished.

Are you ready? The gold rose is thirty dollars. It is "full size" and "unique" because each gold rose begins as an actual American Beauty rose that is saturated in chemicals, then electroplated, "in twenty-four-karat pure gold." How many listeners might have assumed the rose was three thousand dollars? Fortunately, we insisted on saying "thirty dollars."

The key attribute of print media is accuracy. The power of the spoken word is persuasion. If you are hung up on black-and-white "accuracy," I suggest you stick to print media. But if you want to persuade the world, use TV or radio and the power of the human voice. Whatever you do, please don't impose the narrow rules of print media on the limitless possibilities of the spoken word.

Ability is useless unless it's used.

Robert Half

50

You Must Be Present to Win

Andy Carroll walks the sidewalks of the strip in Las Vegas, never noticing what surrounds him. Bathed in unthinkable watts of neon splendor, casinos rise from the earth like palaces in a dream and people walk past him dressed like royalty in the night. Andy Carroll just looks at his watch and yawns.

Hoping to find something to eat, Andy walks into a casino and spies an obscure little sign that says, "You must be present to win." It stops him on the spot. He points to the sign and announces to the room, "That's one of the most poetic things I've ever seen in my life!"

Andy Carroll is a writer learning to live in the now.

Andy knows that "being present" is the key to winning in far more ways than one. Andy is winning friends everywhere due to his ability to "be present" when listening to others. He's making people feel good by giving them his undivided attention. As a writer, Andy has also discovered that using verbs in their present tense is the key to winning the attention of the public in an overcommunicated society. As a result, Andy now writes in the present tense and puts his readers on the scene.

Songwriters and poets often do this instinctively. "Tall and tan and young and lovely, the girl from Ipanema goes walking, and when she passes, each one she passes goes a-a-a-h . . ." "Whose woods these are I think I know. His house is in the village, though; he will not see me stopping here to watch his woods fill up with snow."

The power of writing in the present tense is rooted in Broca's area of the brain. Because Broca's area is activated by verb generation rather than object naming, "I run" (present tense) or "I am running" (present

"The Girl from Ipanema," Vinicius de Moraes, Norman Gimbel, Antonio Carlos Jobim, 1963

"Stopping by Woods on a Snowy Evening," Robert Frost, 1923

progressive) conjures an image far more powerful than "I have run" (present perfect), "I ran" (past), "I had run" (past perfect), or "I will run" (future).

Present tense verbs also gain power from their infrequent usage. The human mind takes delight in the unexpected.

Joe Romano and I step into a fine Italian restaurant called "Onofrio's" and see a sign prominently displayed in the lobby: "This restaurant is highly recommended by the owner." Audacity is another literary tool that leverages the power of the unexpected. Audacious statements have far more impact than those that are predictable.

Are you doing the predictable? Are you writing and speaking in the past and future tense? Are you avoiding audacity for fear that someone might be offended? Are people walking barefoot because you bore the socks off them?

See ch. 21, "Wernicke and Broca," and ch. 30, "Surprising Broca."

Engage the imagination with active voice. In passive voice, the subject of the sentence is acted upon: "The sword is carried by me." In active voice, the subject performs the action: "I carry the sword."

The risk of insult is the price of clarity.

The Wizard

51

Nitroglycerin

ingles, drama, humor, and testimonials are the nitroglycerin of advertising. Used properly, these things have the power to move mountains for you. Handle them carelessly and they'll blow up in your face.

Musical jingles can surprise Broca, but more often they put him to sleep. As you learned in chapter 32, never get caught using a mediocre jingle. If it's not a killer, kill it.

Drama gives us the power to compel by tapping into the customer's imagination. Can you produce a dramatic reenactment that won't be perceived as transparent and contrived? Predictable drama is counterproductive when it's seen by the public as a clumsy attempt to manipulate them. No one likes to feel manipulated.

Humor can sharpen the point of an ad like a whetstone, but it's just as likely to blunt your point and make the ad unproductive. Does your humor reinforce the point of the ad, or is it merely a gratuitous distraction? Often, the customer will remember the humor, but nothing else about the ad. Is your goal to entertain — or to persuade?

See ch. 30, "Surprising Broca," and ch. 32, "A Spoonful of Sugar."

Whether ad lib or scripted, testimonials are simply another form of drama. Though your testimonial may be completely genuine and authentic, unrehearsed and unsolicited, this does not require the public to believe it. If the finished testimonial ad isn't utterly convincing, drop it like a hot rock.

Extreme caution is essential when handling things of great power. "The greater the power, the more difficult the control" is just as true in advertising as in thoroughbred horses, nuclear physics, racing engines, and fame.

The Wizard's advice concerning nitroglycerin: Never attempt to create a musical jingle or to use drama, humor, or testimonials in your ads unless you're prepared to walk away from the effort should the result fall short of the mark. Are you willing to discard a finished ad that misses the bullseye? Or would you feel compelled to use it anyway?

52

The Secret Path to Miraculous Ads

atthew wants a career writing miracle-producing ads, so he goes to college to refine his skills. Journalism instructors teach Matthew to present the facts objectively: "The goal of the journalist is always to inform, never to persuade." Creative writing instructors teach Matthew how to use words to thrill and entertain. Business profs teach him a bit of journalism here, some creative writing there. ✱

Matt graduates with honors and for the next thirty-seven years makes a good living by writing ads that inform and entertain the public. But rarely do Matt's ads persuade.

Unlike news stories and entertainment, ads don't receive the committed attention of the public. Therefore, the ad writer must engage the imagination of an unwilling mind and transfer an entirely new perspective in less than sixty seconds.

Which writer conveys an entirely new perspective in a tight economy of words? Who always opens with a commanding first mental

See "first mental image," "last mental image," p. 117.

1. **Journalism:** The goal of the reporter/newswriter is to present the facts in an objective manner in an attempt to inform, *not* to persuade.

2. **Creative writing:** Novelists and screenwriters assume the committed attention of the public. Their goal is to entertain, *not* to persuade.

3. **Poetry/lyricism:** Poets were among the most highly revered persons in ancient society, much as rock stars are revered in our society today. Nothing, really, has changed. What is a song but poetry set to music? (See ch. 31, "The Ad Writer as Poet.")

✱No college m America of a course called "Persuasive Writing." W... is this?

image and summarizes with stinging simplicity? Who can teach us to write ads that truly persuade?

While the journalist seeks to inform us and the creative writer entertains, it is the poet who changes how we see the world. Using unpredictable words in unusual combinations, the poet seizes the mind with an engaging first mental image, then leads us sharply down her path of words to a stunning last mental image and a whole new way of thinking.

Words are the most powerful force there has ever been. If you will illuminate the mind, win the heart, inspire the public, and change the world, steal a few moments each day to quietly walk the path of poetry. Wandering through that enchanted forest, you'll find the place where miracles begin.

They may forget what you said, but they will never forget how you made them feel.

Carl W. Buechner

53

What Do You See?

emory is formed of images, but not of the images we have seen with our eyes. Memory is formed of the images we've seen in the imagination. For your ads to be effective, they must be recalled when the prospective customer has need of what you sell. Do you know how to make your ads memorable, or are you foolishly attempting to schedule your ads to the precise moment of the customer's need?

The secret of writing memorable ads is to use language that creates a vivid first mental image (FMI) and closes with an equally vivid last mental image (LMI). Notice that I said "mental," not "visual," image. The mind does not easily store and retrieve the images of the eye. The mind recalls the images of the mind — images placed there by words and emotions, images created by language and love and hope and fear and impressions both specific and vague.

An enticing FMI is the essential first step in creating a winning ad, because it determines whether your prospect will continue to listen. An intrusive and intriguing FMI will cause the prospect to abandon the thought she had been thinking. The best FMI plunges the listener into a world of stored memories, both real and imagined. Do your ads do this?

"You are standing in the snow, five and one-half miles above sea level, gazing at a horizon hundreds of miles away." "Whenever Richard Cory went downtown, we people on the pavement looked at him." "She will kiss you like you've never been kissed before." Can you see how these FMIs might entice the listener to continue listening?

In a TV ad, we hear a clear, male voice say, "The Brita water filtration system makes tap water taste great." Notice the weak FMI. Since we cannot easily imagine a "Brita water filtration system," our interest

Don't take my word for it — read it for yourself in the Journal of Cognitive Neuroscience.

See ch. 50, "You Must Be Present to Win."

is not engaged. In this simple sponsor recognition line, the only clear mental image is of great-tasting water, which makes it the obvious FMI. The one-line tag would have been much more effective had they said, "Tap water tastes great when you have a Brita water filtration system." In my rearranged version of the sponsor statement, the first mental image is of great-tasting water and the last mental image is of the listener "having" a Brita water filtration system.

While a good FMI entices the listener to give you her attention, it's a good LMI that causes her to "see" herself doing the thing you wish her to do: ". . . have a Brita water filtration system." A good LMI is more than a call to action; the well-written LMI actually completes the desired action in the mind, creating a mental picture in which the action has already taken place. The only remaining need is to transfer this imagined experience into actual experience.

Remember the Seventh Law of the Advertising Universe: "Engage the imagination, then take it where you will. Where the mind has repeatedly journeyed, the body will surely follow. People go only to places they have already been in their minds."

The greatest of all ad writers is the one who engages your imagination with a vivid first mental image, then uses that image to lead you down the hill, over the river, through the woods, around the corner, and back up the hill to where you began. There's something magical about returning to the first mental image and seeing it from a whole new perspective. If you truly want to study under the masters, listen to the incomparable Paul Harvey and read the poems of Robert Frost.

First mental image (FMI): The initial mental image (see "mental image," p. 70) created by an ad, from which the rest of the ad must flow; the opening scene of the play that will be performed in the imagination.

Last mental image (LMI): The mental image with which an ad ends; the final scene of the play.

Primacy, recency: Words at the beginning of a list are more easily recalled than words in the middle; this is known among psychologists as the *primacy effect*. Words at the end of a list are more easily recalled as well, due to a phenomenon known as the *recency effect*. Primacy and recency make it essential that ads begin and end memorably. Most ad writers, however, bury the point in the middle of the ad and end with predictably dull information such as addresses and phone numbers. This does not surprise Broca. If you want your ad to be memorable, write an ending that does not fit the anticipated schema (see p. 71).

54

Sequencing Mental Images

egard the following ad:

She wakes up Saturday morning at 6:45 and pours herself a cup of coffee. At 7:00, she begins making breakfast for the kids, and by 8:15, she's cheering them on at their soccer game. By 10:30, she's in the back yard working in the garden, and she barely has time to shower before meeting her regular foursome for golf at the country club, where, at precisely 3:46:17 PM, she putts for a birdie on the eighteenth hole. She returns home for another quick shower, and by 5:30 she's slipping into a dress for an evening at the symphony, to be followed by a soiree across town at the home of a friend. (Pause) And what watch does she wear throughout the day, from garden, to golf course, to symphony? Why, a Lady's Rolex, of course. Rolex — the only watch as versatile as the woman who wears one. (Pause) I'm Woody Justice, and I've got a Rolex for you.

Announcer: Your Rolex is waiting patiently for you to come and pick it up — at Justice Jewelers, your official Rolex jeweler, on Highway 65 at Battlefield Road.

Woody: How long will you keep it waiting?

This ad was written as the sequel to the "Mount Everest" ad featured in chapter 9 of *The Wizard of Ads*. Masculine heroism, such as climbing Everest, is easily defined. But how do women define the heroic female? The answer, in a word, is "versatility." Today's heroic female is the one who can "do it all" and still be a woman. Today's heroic female can be as tough or as soft as the situation demands. She can be a gardener, a golfer, a businesswoman, a mom.

The genius of this ad (written by my associate, Trace Shelton) is in its sequencing of mental images and in its ongoing references to time. Long before you know it's an ad for a watch, you hear "6:45,"

Though presented in a format for radio, this ad copy would also work well in a newspaper, TV, or magazine ad.

118

"7:00," "8:15," "10:30" as the ad copy outlines the busy day of our heroic woman. The ad then focuses on her birdie putt with a precise reference, "3:46:17," which refers to not only the number of minutes past the hour but the number of seconds as well. These references help create a deeper awareness of the importance of time in today's world.

Equally important are the mental images elicited by the words in the ad. Through his reference to "Saturday morning" in the opening line, the writer is careful not to reveal whether this woman is employed or is a lady of leisure. Our goal is for both women to feel included. Likewise, we do not know whether she is married or single. We further honor the woman in our assumption that she can buy herself a watch and does not need a man to buy one for her. These are the images seen by the female listener.

See "mental image," p. 70; "first mental image," "last mental image," p. 117.

But what mental images does the typical male listener "see" as he hears this ad? In all likelihood, he sees the woman he loves standing naked under jets of warm, soapy water in the shower. Twice. (Once after gardening and again after golfing.) Though thoroughly innocent and in perfectly good taste, these mental images of female nudity are contained in the ad, nonetheless. The sexual tension is further heightened by the statement, "How long will you keep it waiting?"

Would it surprise you to learn that this ad sells as many Lady's Rolexes to men as it does to women?

I'm not saying this is how we ought to be. I'm saying it's how we are.

ELGIN

ELGIN NATIONAL WATCH CO.

SUPERIOR TO ALL OTHERS IN STYLE, QUALITY and FINISH.

WATCHES

119

55

Calculating the Ad Budget

ost business owners have been taught to budget approximately 5 to 6 percent of total sales for advertising and another 5 to 6 percent for rent, or cost of occupancy. This formula, however, often results in underperformance due to too little being spent on advertising. The business owner who spends only 1 or 2 percent of total sales on cost of occupancy is seriously underspending when only 5 to 6 percent is budgeted for advertising.

The purpose of advertising is to increase the exposure of your business beyond what is provided by your physical location. The business owner who saves money by investing in a weak location will have to advertise much more heavily. A high cost of occupancy for a landmark location is often the least expensive advertising your money can buy.

Although there's no "one size fits all" formula for calculating the correct advertising budget, there is a concise formula for calculating the ad budget for retail businesses, and, in my experience, the formula can be easily adjusted to serve other business categories as well.

The following formula assumes a retail business with a 50 percent gross margin: ✱

:100% markup, see chapter 66, "Banker Talk")

Step 1. Budget 10 to 12 percent of total projected sales for total cost of exposure.

Step 2. Adjust this figure by the store's average markup (above cost of goods sold). If the average markup is 100 percent ("keystone"), then the formula is unadjusted (10–12 percent of projected sales × 100 percent). If the average markup is only 91 percent, then the adjusted budget for total cost of exposure will also be reduced by 9 percent (10–12 percent of projected sales × 91 percent — see?).

Likewise, if the average markup is 150 percent, then the adjusted budget for total cost of exposure would be increased by 50 percent (10–12 percent ¥ 150 percent.)

Step 3. Deduct your cost of occupancy from your adjusted total cost of exposure. The balance is your ad budget. 🖐

	Low budget	High budget	High budget	
	Medium markup	Medium markup	Low markup	High markup
Total annual sales	$1,000,000 × 10%	$1,000,000 × 12%	$1,000,000 × 12%	$1,000,000 × 12%
Budget for total cost of exposure (occupancy + advertising)	100,000	120,000	120,000	120,000
Average markup	× 92%	× 92%	× 61%	× 117%
Adjusted budget for total cost of exposure	92,000	110,400	73,200	140,400
Cost of occupancy	−36,000	−36,000	−36,000	−36,000
AD BUDGET	$56,000	$74,400	$37,200	$104,400

See how markup affects the ad budget?

121

56

Cost per What?

am discussing the future of radio with three executives from one of America's most progressive broadcast groups when we're interrupted by my operations manager: "That sales rep you've been waiting to hear from is on line fourteen." "Thanks, Trish, tell him I'll be right with him." I ask Geoff, John, and Dennis to excuse me for a moment because I need to increase a client's radio presence in a major northern city. "No problem," they say, laughing. "It'll be interesting to watch an advertising buyer at work."

When my phone conversation is over, a gloom seems to have settled over my friends. John Cullen looks as though he might be about to cry. His normally booming voice is almost a whisper as he says, "What did we just see happen?" Not understanding what he means, I stare at him blankly.

Then Geoff Armstrong speaks up. "It looked like you were offering to increase your spending by 50 percent if the rep could show you a schedule that would give you 50 percent more weekly frequency." Still staring blankly, I nod in the affirmative.

Now John speaks again: "It sounded like the sales rep was trying to force you into a conversation about spot rates and cost per point."

Now I see what's troubling them. I explain, "I was talking 'reach and frequency,' and the sales rep was talking 'cost per point.' Is that what's got you bothered?" All three heads begin nodding slowly, in unison.

See "reach," "frequency," p. 131.

Geoff, John, and Dennis are troubled because they know that advertising schedules should be proposed and considered according to their reach and frequency. That's how advertising works. Advertisers who buy gross rating points will nearly always reach too many people with too little frequency.

When a media buyer buys one hundred gross rating points, what has he done? Does he reach 100 percent of the city one time each? Fifty percent of the city twice? Twenty-five percent of the city four times? Ten percent ten times, or a single percent one hundred times? It's almost impossible to say. Yet each of these schedules will look exactly the same in terms of gross rating points.

Which is better? (1) A schedule that reaches 100 percent of the city and persuades them 10 percent of the way? or (2) a schedule that reaches 10 percent of the city and persuades them 100 percent of the way? Both schedules provide exactly the same number of gross rating points and cost the same amount of money. The only difference is that the second plan works and the first one doesn't. Successful advertising is the result of good writing and strong frequency.

See "media dominance," p. 107.

Are you buying too much reach and too little frequency with your ad budget? Have you bought into the myth of "media mix"? Are your ads underproducing due to fragmented placement and poor scheduling?

See ch. 3, "Dead Cows Everywhere."

Overtargeting: The common practice of spending too much money in a misguided effort to "reach the right person," driven by the mistaken assumption that decisions are made in a vacuum. The key to success in advertising is to deeply impress whoever you reach, then count on those persons to be your ambassadors or "inside champions." (See "word-of-mouth advertising," p. 128; ch. 3, "Dead Cows Everywhere.")

By the way, that rep in the major northern market hasn't gotten back to me yet. The word on the street is that he's frustrated with me because I don't know how to buy advertising.

57

The Goose and the Gander

"What's good for the goose is good for the gander" might be true in goose ranching, but it's not a valid concept in business. Strategies, concepts, and technologies that are proven winners for big companies are often counterproductive for smaller ones. What's good for the big corporate goose can be poison to the independent gander.

Three examples of goose food/gander poison are the concepts of a media mix in advertising, math-based goal setting, and long-range planning. There's a lot of truth in the religion of media mix, but it is a truth inappropriate for the small business owner. The idea of a media mix assumes that your advertising budget is adequate to do a good job in each part of the mix. Coke, Pepsi, Chevrolet, Procter & Gamble, and the other big boys are able to accomplish a media mix without being forced to compromise any part of it. They can mix radio, television, newspaper, magazines, and skywriting without having to do anything halfway.

See ch. 3, "Dead Cows Everywhere."

Is this true of your company? Do you have this kind of budget? If not, I recommend that you do one thing well rather than two things badly. You may be able to do two things well, but I've never worked with a company that could do three things well. But then I've never worked with anyone who had more than a couple of million dollars to spend on advertising.

Math-based goal setting provides structure and direction for large companies that need a common denominator to measure their own progress against that of their competitors, and to compare the progress of different divisions within their own company. Their goals involve numbers and more numbers. Numbers everywhere: percentage growth targets tied to calendar dates, sales goals tied to bonus plans, ratios of new stores opened to old stores closed, and this week's stock price compared with last week's. While numbers might speak to the soul of corporations and the needs of stockholders, they play a much smaller part in the drama of privately held companies and independent business owners.

Long-range planning may be the goose that lays the golden eggs for big companies, but it can be the wild goose of the proverbial chase for small ones. The only advantage of smallness in business is the ability to respond quickly to the opportunities of a changing marketplace. You can get your goose cooked if you commit to an inflexible, long-range plan in a small, nimble company! Rarely have I seen a small-business five-year plan that had any value at the end of eighteen months.

My friend Joe Romano, a gifted professional planner, says, "The flexibility of a plan must increase in direct proportion to the smallness of the company." Improperly done, long-range planning is just one more pitiful attempt to turn life into a predictable science.

58

Radio Scheduling

he pivotal question in any discussion of radio scheduling is "How will you measure success?" Do you plan to use radio to (1) draw a crowd to your special event, or (2) make the name of your company a household word?

If you're going on radio to promote a special event, please know that you're using the world's champion marathon runner to run a fifty-yard dash. It's true that newspaper ads often outperform radio ads in the short term, but you should never assume that radio can't draw a crowd: every radio employee in America has seen his station attract massive crowds to special events. (A marathon runner can run a respectable fifty-yard dash — it's just not the highest and best use of his talents.)

See ch. 4
Long Is t'

To advertise a special event on radio, you should schedule an ad to air just before your event begins, then move backward in time, scheduling one spot per hour until you've run out of ad budget. Generally, a special event schedule should be at least thirteen spots per day, 6 AM–7 PM,* for at least five days prior to the event. Sixty-five spots should be considered an absolute minimum schedule on each of the stations you plan to use. (If you can persuade a station's program director to let you air two spots per hour, then schedule two spots per hour. The goal is to increase the ratio of ad repetition to listener sleep.)

The real power of radio, however, is long-term memory, or "top of mind awareness." Smart advertisers are those who set out to win the customer's heart long before she needs their product. Their only goal is to be the company she thinks of first and feels the best about whenever her need arises. Smart advertisers make no attempt to predict

See "critical equation," p. 129.

*If you have the available budget, add a spot per hour during the evening and overnight hours for a total of 24 spots per day per station

the moment of the customer's need but buy enough repetition to ensure they will immediately spring to mind whenever such need arises.

To become a household word, you must buy at least twenty-one radio ads per week (plus or minus two ads), per station, 6 AM to 7 PM or 8 PM,** fifty-two weeks per year, on as many stations as you can afford. Plan to endure minimal results during the first eight to thirteen weeks of your schedule. This is known as the "chickening-out period," when you will probably spend a lot more on radio advertising than you will see in results.

* If the TV news airs at 10 pm, the hours before 7 pm will be radio prime. If the news airs at 11 pm, then radio prime is extended to 8 pm.

Establishing echoic retention: Variables are (1) power of message (emotional voltage), (2) repetition (frequency), and (3) consistency.

When you have a commitment to 52-week consistency and an average message, a 3 frequency can be established with nearly two-thirds of the weekly cume on most radio stations with 21 ads a week (plus or minus two ads), 6 AM–7 PM (6 AM–8 PM if the late evening news on television is at 11 PM instead of 10 PM).

Horizontal Scheduling

When faced with too large a station and too small a budget, consider buying a "station within the station." Example: Schedule twenty-one spots per week, fifty-two weeks per year, between the hours of 7 PM and midnight, and you will typically reach less than half the station's total weekly audience, but you will have good repetition with the segment you're reaching. The schedule will also be dramatically less

See "media dominance," p. 107.

expensive than a comparable daytime schedule. Personally, I'm convinced that the greatest advertising bargain in America is radio advertising between 7 PM and 6 AM. It's wonderfully underpriced.

Vertical Scheduling

Another successful scheduling technique is to buy a "vertical" schedule on Sundays, airing one spot per hour for at least thirteen consecutive hours, fifty-two weeks a year. Though radio listenership is somewhat lower on Sundays than on weekdays, rates are also less expensive. Like the 7 PM-to-midnight schedule discussed above, a vertical Sunday schedule gives you a "station within the station" and allows for solid repetition with at least a certain percentage of the station's total audience. (I've often bought late nights and Sundays only.)

What about OES?

"OES" refers to a particular mathematical formula used in conjunction with a station's Arbitron ratings to produce what is called *optimum effective scheduling*. Although OES is widely used by some of the

Word-of-mouth advertising is created when people talk about things that have impressed them deeply — whether positive or negative. Are you impressing the public with ads that have impact and meaning? Are you impressing your customers with the world inside your door? (See ch. 64, "The World Inside Your Door," and ch. 3, "Dead Cows Everywhere.")

brightest minds in radio, I generally find OES schedules to be too few spots per week for a special event, and too many spots per week when the advertiser is committed to the long term. The one factor not taken into consideration in the OES formula is the advertiser's term of commitment.

Critical equation: The ratio of ad repetition to listener sleep. Assuming an average message, the individual listener needs to hear the identical ad 3 times within each 7 nights' sleep.

Variables: The formula assumes that the message is of average impact and that the majority of the audience is not currently in the market for the product. Other variables are the number of years of repetition and the strength of competitors.

Change your ad when the listener has been exposed to the identical information 12–20 times.

Radio is word-of-mouth advertising evolved to its highest level.

Tom Haymond

ADIO SERVICE

59

Television Scheduling

In television, you generally get what you pay for. Though I know of no real way to beat the system, most television stations and cable systems will treat you fairly. However, there are a couple of mistakes you definitely *don't* want to make:

1. Never buy a broad rotator. TV stations and cable systems will offer dramatically reduced rates in return for the freedom to place your ads within broad windows in their daily schedule. Though the rates may look attractive, such schedules make it virtually impossible to reach viewers with enough repetition to be effective. The greatest likelihood is that you will reach an enormous number of different people approximately one time each. Although it's possible to see results using a broad rotator, it's never the highest or best use of your money.

2. Don't assume the viewer is loyal to a particular station. Although television viewers may have loyalty to a particular TV show, they rarely have loyalty to the station. Even when viewers are loyal to a particular newscast, it's the show to which they are responding, not the station. It's a tragic mistake to believe that a particular station's audience is intrinsically different from the audience of another. The show is what attracts birds of a feather, not the station.

There are four things to remember when placing a television schedule:

1. Always schedule horizontally. The best way to ensure that you'll reach the same person with a second and third repetition of your ad is to buy advertising in the same television show over and over again.

2. "Roadblock" when your ads have a high impact quotient. When your ad is irresistible and you need to make sure that you're reaching the largest number of people that you possibly can, try roadblocking at a particular time each day — buy fixed-position ads to air simultaneously on every station in town. (A viewer might run from your roadblock, but he can't hide.) Roadblocking is most common during the late evening news.

3. Find a sales rep who will keep your best interest in mind. Things can change quickly in television, and a sales rep who's watching out for you is worth his weight in gold.

4. Use cable for what cable does best. When the city is too large and your budget is too small, "shrink the city" by buying only those cable zones in which you have store locations. The primary advantage of cable advertising is in its ability to limit the geographic distribution of your ads. This allows you to buy a lower reach with greater frequency than you could have purchased from a broadcast facility.

Reach: The total number of different people reached by an ad campaign.

Frequency: The number of times your ad will reach the same person in a given period.

60

Seeing Yourself Real

Subject: A shot of adrenaline
Date: Wed, 03 Mar 1999 10:54:31 -0500
From: "Sean McNally" <mcnally@staffnet.com>
To: <roy@rhw.com>

Roy,

I just wanted to say THANK YOU!!! for The Wizard of Ads. I read an article about it in one of the myriad business magazines & it caught my attention. My wife proceeded to get it for me for Christmas & I had read it cover to cover 2 days later. It has revolutionized the way I am promoting my T-shirt screen printing business. I shave my head, have 6 earrings and a little scruff of a beard on my chin (needless to say, I stand out in the local Chamber of Commerce meetings in our small town). Well, I decided not to let that hinder my business, because it's who I am! We have recently begun to run ads with my picture asking things like "Could a guy like this know anything about 'old fashioned' customer service? You might be surprised," and it's working. People are coming up to me in meetings (the same ones that I have been attending for the past year) and they've seen the ad & want to work with me. Your book was like a clear sound in a noisy room & thank God I heard it!!!

Thanks again

God Bless

Sean McNally

Subject: Ad-renaline

Date: Thu, 04 Mar 1999 09:17:47 +0000

From: Roy Williams <roy@rhw.com>

Organization: Roy H. Williams Marketing

To: Sean McNally <mcnally@staffnet.com>

Sean,

I'm flattered, thrilled, honored, and delighted that
my book inspired you to create such extraordinary
ads! With your permission, I'd like to use the
campaign you've created as an example of what I mean
when I say, "The secret of successful advertising is
to uncover the story that is uniquely and
wonderfully your own, and then tell that story in
the most compelling way possible."

See ch. 11, "Digging
for the Diamond."

What amazes me most is that you were able to do this
for yourself! Most of us don't "see ourselves real"
when we look in the mirror. Not only do you have the
courage to see yourself real, you have the creative
gift of expressing yourself in a most compelling
fashion.

Sean, you da'Man!

Roy H. Williams

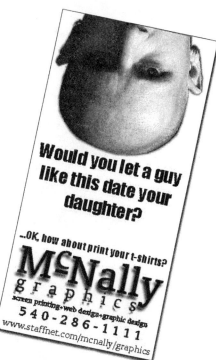

133

61

Change Is Inevitable, Growth Is Optional

Although there are tens of thousands of seemingly contradictory laws and ordinances in America, a close examination will reveal that our entire system of jurisprudence is based on just a few recurrent principles that the courts apply daily in every area of our lives.

If a man and a woman present themselves as husband and wife for a certain period of years, then our laws consider them to be legally married, though they've neither applied for a marriage license nor participated in any ceremony. All it takes to be legally married in America is to subscribe to a few magazines in the name of "Mr. and Mrs." and write checks on a joint checking account. In effect, American law says, "You say you're married? Okay, you're married."

Likewise, there is a law in real estate that says if you willingly allow a neighbor to cut across the corner of your property for a certain number of years, then the neighbor ultimately gains a legal right to that corner and can no longer be barred from using the shortcut. The willful and ongoing lack of action by the landowner is interpreted by the courts to be implied permission.

With these examples in mind, can you anticipate the court's ruling in an instance when an author has watched others reprint his work for a number of years and never once taken action to enforce his copyrights? Will he now be allowed to enforce them?

The point that I'm trying to make is simply this: A foolish student memorizes formulas. A wise one understands them.

Look for hard and fast rules and you're likely to live a frustrated life, but wrap your mind around life's recurrent principles and you'll be delighted to see how constantly they apply in our ever-changing world.

Wisdom doesn't live in a set of rules, but in the ongoing application of the principles behind them. Rules will change with circumstances, but principles are constant forever.

Wisdom is the principal thing;
therefore get wisdom: and with
all thy getting get understanding.

Solomon

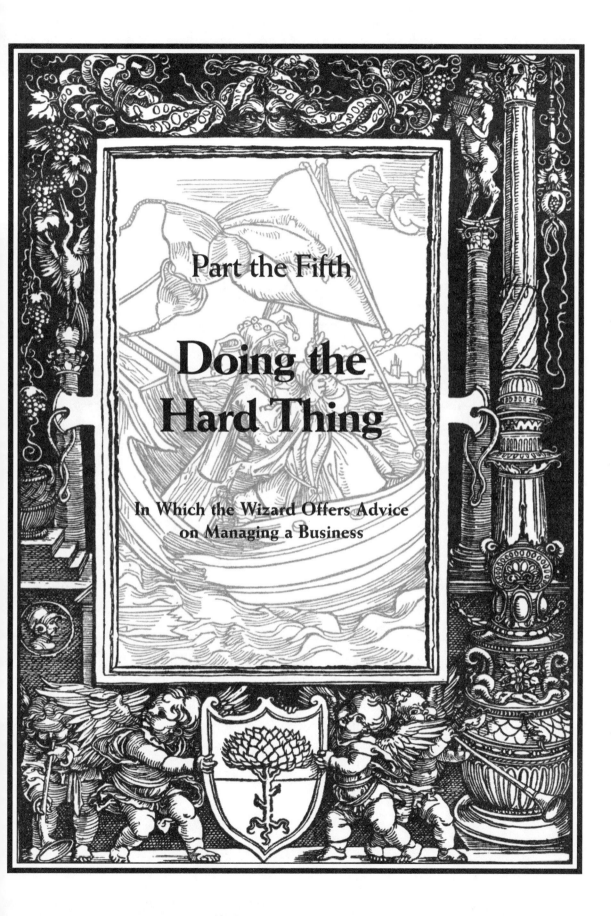

Part the Fifth

Doing the
Hard Thing

In Which the Wizard Offers Advice
on Managing a Business

62

Huebner's First Rule of Mountaineering: Climb with Passion

I suppose it's because I know quite a few highly successful business owners that interviewers often ask me, "What do successful entrepreneurs all have in common? What is it that makes them different?"

Each time I'm asked the question, I respond with exactly the same answer: "Successful entrepreneurs are those who have a passion for their business and the money to survive their mistakes. I've occasionally seen success happen without sufficient funding, but I've never once seen it happen without passion."

If a business is a machine, an engine for making money, then passion is simply emotional gasoline, providing the indispensable energies of optimism, creativity, and tenacity. A money-making business is simply the result of a properly channeled passion.

When you first read Jim Huebner's Six Rules of Mountaineering, along with his comment that he suspected "they could also apply to advertising," were you surprised to read that the first rule of mountaineering is "Climb with passion"?

Huebner's Six Rules
of Mountaineering:
See pp. 37–38.

Passion is essential to every climber who hopes to reach the summit. Summits require passion, regardless of whether they are physical summits or metaphorical ones. The fact that summits demand passion is an immutable law of the universe. It's true not only in mountain climbing and business, but in relationships, agriculture, medicine, and theology as well. It's true in every branch of human endeavor.

The truth must always be true. It simply cannot be otherwise.

Always climb with passion.

63

The Three Worlds of Business:
1. The World Outside Your Door

Think about the people in your city who don't do business with you: Is it because they don't know about you? Or is it because they do?

The customer's expectations and preconceptions can be found in the World Outside Your Door. This is where your reputation lives in the hearts of the people. What is the typical customer's predisposition toward you? What expectations does he have? How well are you really known and how much of what is known is real?

The World Outside Your Door is also where media dominance is established. Will this be accomplished by you or by your competitor?

Simply put, the World Outside Your Door is the world of advertising, the place where success begins.

But it definitely doesn't end there.

See "media dominance," p. 107.

64

The Three Worlds of Business:
2. The World Inside Your Door

The World Inside Your Door is the world of the customer's experience: the place where you must make good on all the bold promises you've made in your ads. How well do you deliver on those promises?

Eyes, ears, nose, and skin enter the World Inside Your Door. How pleasant are the signals they receive? Regardless of whether your customer steps into a physical store or merely contacts you by phone or Internet, advertising is finished the moment that contact is made.

In an instant, the eyes of the customer assess your merchandise and lighting. What impact do these make? Meanwhile, the customer's ears receive the acoustical signature of your wall covering, floor covering, and ceiling. Is there music in the air, or is the store filled with the energy of customer noise? (Either is fine, as long as it's a distinctive acoustic signature you've created as part of the overall customer experience.) Is the nose greeted by intentional smells or accidental ones? Is the skin touched by a whispering breeze at an inviting temperature, or does the customer feel the store to be a little stuffy and uncomfortable?

Don't expect advertising to fix problems inside your door. If there's a deficiency in the quality of your customer's experience, fix it!

See ch. 67, "Have You Fixed the Leak in Your Boat?" and ch. 80, "Would You Believe Twenty-Six to One?"

Lighting

There's a profound difference between illumination and lighting. Which do you employ? Illumination is a streetlight at an intersection; lighting is the spotlight on a stage. Illumination is the homogenized ocean of light in a cafeteria; lighting is the candle on your table in a restaurant. Illumination is the sterile wash of fluorescent bulbs in a discount store; lighting is the carefully constructed play of highlight and shadow at Abercrombie & Fitch. (If a mall near you has an Abercrombie & Fitch, go take a look at the lighting and you'll see exactly what I mean.)

Merchandising

"Selection" is a hundred dresses hung on a circular rack. "Merchandising" is a model walking the runway at a fashion show. Selection is a car lot with two hundred cars; merchandising is one car, polished like a diamond, on a rotating platform lit by 50,000 watts of light under a night sky. When you scan the menu in a restaurant, that's selection. When a waiter lowers a covered dish and whisks the lid off with a flourish to reveal the wonderful desserts inside, that's merchandising.

Salespeople

I'm questioning Jon Silva about the liberal way he pays his staff; he looks at me quizzically and says, "Hey, it's not what you pay 'em — it's what they cost you." Sensing a story, I encourage my friend to explain.

"A few years ago," says Jon, "I saw one of my salespeople watching an old gentleman who was looking at jewelry in our window. She was delighted when he walked into the store and announced, 'I'd like to see the jade bracelet in the window, please.' She scurried over to the window, retrieved the bracelet and brought it to him. Seeing that the price was only $400, he said, 'I'll take it.' I continued watching them from across the store until she placed his gift-wrapped package into a bag and thanked him for coming in. Seeing that the old gentleman was about to leave, I walked over and said, 'I see that you bought the marvelous jade bracelet in the window. Is it for her birthday or your anniversary?' He told me that it was to be a gift for his wife on their wedding anniversary. 'I guarantee she's going to love it,' I said. 'That's really a very special bracelet, and I can promise you that none of her friends has ever seen anything like it. Before you

See "personal experience factor," p. 105.

leave, let me show you a necklace that goes just perfectly with it. Maybe some day you'll want to add it to the bracelet.'

"The old fellow followed me over to a showcase, where I presented an $8,500 necklace over my arm and said, 'If you ever want to take her breath away and see her cry, just give her this.' Five minutes later, he was walking out the door with a second package in the bag, and that's only because it took us five minutes to wrap the necklace. He bought it immediately.

"That girl was about to let the old gentleman leave without ever showing him the necklace. The fact that she was paid only eight dollars an hour is much less important than the fact she nearly cost me eighty-five hundred."

Jon showed me the letter he received from the old man's wife:

Dear Mr. Silva,

I have known for thirty-two years that my husband's secret fantasy was to startle me with a magnificent gift, yet not once have I ever received anything that remotely compares to the necklace Harry bought for me in your store. You see, my Harry is a man of considerable means, but he has always been fearful that I might pretend to like an expensive gift when I actually did not care for it. Thank you! Thank you! Thank you for convincing Harry that I would be truly delighted with the necklace! I have waited thirty-two long years for you to finally cross his path.

I only wish you could have seen his face when I gasped and began to cry! When I saw how startled he was, Harry told me what you had said that made him buy the necklace, and then we both laughed and laughed and laughed until we had to sit on the floor. Thank you for making this the happiest anniversary any two people have ever had.

Very Sincerely and Appreciatively Yours,

Millie Fonseca

P.S. Harry has promised me that he will never again shop at any jewelry store but yours.

"You see," said Jon, "it's really not what you pay 'em that matters. It's what they cost you." 🐜

Value: The difference between the anticipated price and the marked price. If the marked price is lower than the anticipated price, the value is perceived as good. If the marked price is higher than the anticipated price, the value is perceived as poor. (There is no profit in lowering the marked price; you must raise the anticipated price!)

65

The Three Worlds of Business:
3. The World of the Executive Office

Earthquakes happen when seismic waves travel outward from an epicenter to literally shake the world. Likewise, businessquakes begin in the office of a CEO and spread from department to department, shaking both paradigm and tradition until the size and shape of the company finally fits the vision of the CEO.

Some businessquakes are the genesis of a brilliant future; others result in bankruptcy. But at the epicenter of every one of them is the chair of a chief executive officer. The quality of the decisions made in that chair is ultimately revealed in the long-term profitability of the company.

To understand a CEO's vision, you need only visit the company. Whom to hire, how much to pay, where to be located, hours of operation, product pricing, merchandising, staff training and motivation are all the result of businessquakes in the mind of the CEO. From there, the ever-spreading ripples create the world of the customer's experience, then continue outward until they are revealed in the company's advertising, forever telling the story that is uniquely and wonderfully their own.

See ch. 11, "Digging for the Diamond."

3/7/99 J. Peterman Founder Is Fired
© The Associated Press TIM WHITMIRE
Lexington, Ky. (AP)

I can't believe this Internet news flash — they took John Peterman's company away from him. He started with nothing but his fingers crossed and built his catalog to more than $70 million in annual revenue, in barely a decade. His new stores were generating more than $500 a square foot, the gold standard in American retail. John was a visionary genius who lost his company because he simply didn't know enough "banker talk."

143

66

Banker Talk

"The communication gap that exists between bankers and business owners," says Tom Bailey, president of Brentwood Bank in Pittsburgh, "is due to the fact that bankers see everything from exactly a reverse perspective. When a bank president talks about his bank's assets and liabilities, you probably assume the bank's assets to be money, right? Well, in banking, the money our depositors give us is actually considered to be a liability. When you deposit money into my bank and I give you a deposit receipt, that's like an IOU. Any time you ask for your money, I've got to be ready to pay it back with interest. In banking, it's actually the loans that are considered to be a bank's assets, not its deposits. This is just one example of how bankers tend to see things backwards from business owners."

The secret of borrowing money is understanding how bankers view the world. When you've learned to answer all your banker's questions in accounting terms (the banker's native tongue), you're a lot more likely to get the loan you'll need to survive the rapid growth that occurs when your company experiences breakthrough.

Bankers tend to have greater confidence in the business owner who keeps at least one finger on the financial ratios of the business and can intelligently discuss how the business is performing in each of six critical areas, but not even bankers look at ratios in absolute terms:

"Ratios in absolute terms aren't nearly as meaningful as they are in relative terms," says Frost Bank vice president Clay Cary. "How your company compares with others in your industry is important, but probably the best use of ratios as a tool is for comparison of your company from one period to the next. The changes in your ratios and the reasons for those changes are what really interest a banker."

Ratios

These are the six basic mathematical relationships you need to understand to be able to speak to bankers in their native tongue:

1. Current ratio measures the liquid assets available to meet all debts falling due within 365 days. The higher the current ratio, the greater the ability of your firm to pay its bills.

Current Assets ÷ Current Liabilities = Current Ratio

Example: If you have a current ratio of 1.5, this means a year's debts could be paid one and one-half times by current assets.

2. Quick ratio is like the current ratio, except that inventories are deducted from assets prior to being divided by liabilities.

(Current Assets – Inventories) ÷ Current Liabilities = Quick Ratio

Since inventory is probably less liquid than other current assets, the quick ratio provides a more accurate picture of your firm's ability to meet its short-term debts.

3. Average collection period ratio is an indicator of how long your company must wait on its receivables.

(Accounts & Notes Receivable × Days in Year) ÷ Annual Credit Sales = Days

Example: If the ratio comes out to fifty-four days, and your credit policy offers thirty-day terms, this means you are collecting your typical receivable twenty-four days after the due date. This stuff matters.

If your average collection time is getting longer, your customers may be paying more slowly because they're having financial problems, or you may not be staying on top of your collection process. Collecting your average receivable a few days earlier can really have a positive impact on your business's cash position or reduce the amount you have to borrow, and conversely, a slowdown can hurt a lot. Here, time really *is* money.

4. Inventory turnover ratio indicates the efficiency of your company's inventory management. Interpreting this ratio can be tricky, since a high ratio may be caused by extremely good inventory management or by levels of inventory that are far too low, meaning that you're too often out of stock on fast-moving items. A low ratio indicates that you've bought too many items that are slow to sell.

(Beginning Inventory + Ending Inventory) ÷ 2 = Average Inventory

Cost of Goods Sold ÷ Average Inventory = Inventory Turnover Ratio

If the turnover ratio turns out to be 2, this means your company sells its total stock of goods twice in one period. Compare with industry averages to see whether your ratio is in line. (Specific industry averages for inventory turnover and most of these other ratios are published regularly by Dun and Bradstreet.)

5. Turnover of working capital ratio measures how actively your working capital is functioning in terms of sales. "Working capital" is all assets that can be converted into operating funds within a year.

Current Assets – Current Liabilities = Working Capital

Net Assets ÷ Working Capital = Turnover of Working Capital

A low ratio means that working capital is not being used efficiently; a high ratio suggests a possible vulnerability to creditors. (Again, check the Dun and Bradstreet averages for your specific industry to see what your target ratio should be.)

6. Debt-to-equity ratio is an indicator of the investment of the lender and other creditors relative to the investment of the owners.

Debt ÷ Equity = Debt-to-Equity Ratio

A high ratio indicates that the business is financed mostly through borrowed funds. A low ratio indicates that the owners have invested heavily in the business. Although different types of businesses do have different standards for debt-to-equity, generally speaking, a high ratio relative to your peers means you will be seen as a higher risk to a banker.

The debt-to-equity ratio is used by lenders as an indicator of your company's ability to weather a storm. Generally, a company with very little relative equity will have a harder time surviving a downturn than will a company with greater equity. Also, all borrowing comes at a cost, so a company that has more debt generally has to pay more interest and is therefore less profitable than its competitors, all other things being equal. Additionally, if your debt level is already high, you will be less likely to borrow additional money to take advantage of new opportunities. Debt-to-equity is a ratio that bankers look at closely.

Clay Cary adds: "One thing small businesses neglect is the quality of their financial statements. Most business owners operate their companies based on a few key indicators that are important to them — maybe daily sales or gross margins or receivables collection or cash position — and they don't pay too much attention to the financial statement as a whole, particularly the balance sheet. You don't have to pay an expensive CPA firm to do an audit, but your financial statement should be prepared by someone who fully understands accounting. If your banker doesn't feel he can rely on the accuracy of the information you're providing, it's difficult to loan money regardless of how comfortable he is with the other loan decision factors. If the financial statement doesn't add up or isn't prepared on a basis that is consistent with basic accounting or tax standards, or if you don't understand your own company's information, you'll immediately lose creditability in the eyes of your banker."

Definitions

Here are some other business terms you should probably know:

cash flow: traditionally, net income plus depreciation and other noncash expenses; a measure of a company's ability over time to meet its debt obligations and fixed asset replacement needs.

close rate: the percentage of your selling opportunities that result in a sale. The national average close rate is 22 percent.

gross margin: the difference between the selling price and the cost, expressed as a percentage of the selling price. If the selling price is $1.50 and cost is $1.00, the gross margin is 33 percent.

gross profit: total sales minus cost of goods sold. This tells you the markup on your cost.

markup: the difference between the selling price and the cost, expressed as a percentage of the cost. If the selling price is $1.50 and cost is $1.00, the markup is 50 percent.

net profit: gross profit minus overhead, taxes, and other expenses — the "bottom line."

operating cash flow: the changes in balance sheet accounts that result in a change in the cash account. When it's positive, there's more in your bank account than when you started; when negative, there's less. This is what people commonly mean when they say cash flow, but it's a better measure of short-term business viability than long-term.

Capitalism is the worst economic system ever invented, except for all the others.

(Something Winston Churchill didn't quite say, but would have if he had thought of it before the Wizard)

67

Have You Fixed the Leak in Your Boat?

egardless of what they might tell you, only three in ten shoppers are "just looking." Statistically, seven of them are hoping to buy today, and they contacted you because they're hoping to buy from you. It's that simple.

These same statistics tell us the average salesperson will close only 22 percent of his selling opportunities.* This means that given ten selling opportunities, the average salesperson will close only two people — yet seven of the ten were *hoping* to buy!

To increase your sales volume by 50 percent, all you need to do is transfer confidence to just one of the five disappointed customers who were hoping to buy. If your sales team can transfer confidence to *two* of the five hopeful but unsold people, your sales volume will double — with zero increase in selling opportunities. All you need to do is sell four out of ten! Your sales team doesn't have to be perfect; it just needs to be better than average. Nobody gets rich selling two out of ten.

If you're looking for a quick payoff, don't gamble your hard-earned money on short-term advertising. The odds simply aren't in your favor. Invest those dollars in sales training instead. Then, when you've fixed the leak in your boat, you can rev up the motor of advertising, and it'll take you wherever you want to go.

So what'll it be? Are you going to look for a more powerful engine, or are you going to fix the leak in your boat?

See ch. 64, "The World Inside Your Door."

*Most business owners mistakenly believe their salespeople close 40-70% of all selling opportunities. Strict & objective counting usually proves otherwise.

Close rate: The percentage of your selling opportunities that result in a sale.

68

Not So Stupid

I liked your memo about the fallacies of deep discounting," said Joe, "But the magic words of retail aren't 'profit margin.' The magic words of retail are 'inventory turn.' It isn't so critical how much you make on an item. What's critical is how often you make it."

See "inven turnover p. 146.

One of my best friends, Joe Romano, is the CEO of Scull and Company, a retail consulting firm that has been guiding business owners to financial greatness since 1922. Joe is easily one of the top ten authorities in America on the subject of business finance, and he was on the phone to explain to me more fully the mysteries of profit margin and inventory turn. I was all ears.

"Take Sam's Club as an example," said Joe. "While the average retailer sells his inventory only once each year, Sam's Club sells the entire inventory in each of their warehouses twelve times a year. Not a bad trick, considering they've been building new warehouses every eleven days since 1983!"

I was incredulous. "Joe, are you telling me that Sam's makes so much money that they can buy several acres of prime real estate and build a gigantic warehouse and fill it with millions of dollars worth of inventory every eleven days?"

"Yes, they're making that kind of money, but it's due to the magic of inventory turn. Sam's adds only a 15 percent markup on each item in the store, but they'll sell and reorder that item twelve times a year. This means that during the same year it takes the average retailer to make a one-dollar markup on his investment of one dollar, Sam's Club invests that same dollar and makes a markup of fifteen cents, twelve times. That's a dollar and eighty cents annual return on a one-dollar investment — nearly double the return on investment experienced by the average retailer in America."

"So I guess you're saying that low markup strategies can work after all?"

"You haven't heard the best part," said Joe. "Since they've got great credit, Sam's Club can get payment terms of ninety days from each of their suppliers. This means that Sam's will sell an item three times, at a 15 percent markup each time, before they have to pay for that item even once. Sam's will have deposited three dollars forty-five cents in the bank before they are obligated to pay the first dollar! Considering that they're selling a multimillion-dollar inventory three times before they have to pay for it even once, does it still surprise you that they have the money to build a new store every eleven days?"

There was a long silence on the phone while I digested what Joe had told me. After a minute or so, Joe snapped me back into the conversation with a question: "What are the magic words of retail?"

"The magic words are 'inventory turn,' Joe."

Just before he had to go, my friend said, "There may still be hope for you as a consultant after all."

Thanks, Joe. I'm keeping my fingers crossed.

69

Who's Buying from Sam? I Am!

"Line 14," says the FedEx man from the front seat of his shiny truck. I've been waiting for this package since yesterday, so I frantically scribble my signature on his clipboard. "Have a good one," he shouts over the noise of the engine. I hurry toward my office.

Yesterday, Ed Ryan called to say, "I'm overnighting you the most fabulous book on selling I've ever read." Ed is the editor of a prestigious magazine, so I was intrigued. "It'll be there in the morning," said Ed. "Gotta go." A click and a dial tone.

Ed is not easily excitable, so I've cleared the morning on my calendar to wait for the FedEx truck on the front steps of my office. Package now in hand, I step inside and am five steps down the hallway shouting, "Hold my calls, Trish! I'll be out till noon." The cardboard package is open even before my office door has closed behind me. I stare in disbelief: *Green Eggs and Ham,* by Dr. Seuss. "Ed Ryan will pay for this," I mutter.

But Seuss books are whimsically seductive, and part of me is still seven years old. Unconsciously, I begin to read, and then suddenly I am ashamed of my anger. Ed Ryan isn't a practical joker; he's a genius. *Green Eggs and Ham* is nothing less than the story of the greatest salesman who never lived: the mythical, immortal, and legendary Sam-I-am. "Will you eat them in a box? Would you eat them with a fox? Would you? Could you? In a car? Eat them! Eat them! Here they are!"

Sam-I-am asks the customer no less than sixteen times to try his green eggs and ham, because Sam-I-am knows the average sale is made when the customer has been asked five times whether he would like to examine a product. The average salesperson will ask only twice.

When customers tell your salespeople they're "just looking," what they're often really saying is, "I don't have any questions yet. Check with me later." Yet few salespeople ever check back with a customer who is "just looking."

A recent national survey tells us that 67 percent of all shoppers intend to return home with the item for which they are shopping, yet only 24 percent actually manage to do so. The other 43 percent tell your salespeople that they're "just looking," and your salespeople let them leave your store disappointed and empty-handed.

Is the fear of being perceived as "pesky" causing your salespeople to deliver poor service to your customers? Are your salespeople expecting the customer to walk over to them and say, "I'm not just looking anymore. Now I'm ready to ask questions"? If you think this may be happening, I suggest that you buy all your salespeople their own copies of *Green Eggs and Ham* and tell them to pay special attention to the end of the story, where the previously reluctant customer exclaims with wide-eyed excitement, "I do so like green eggs and ham! Thank you! Thank you, Sam-I-am!"

See ch. 67, "Have You Fixed the Leak in Your Boat?"

A clerk is the the one who says, "Will that be all?" without ever once looking you in the eye; a sales professional will pause to look up from the cash register and say, with a genuine smile, "We're really glad you took the time to shop with us today, and we hope you'll come again, soon."

Is your company training sales professionals, or clerks?

Trivia: A publisher for Random House bet Dr. Suess $50 that he couldn't write a book using just 50 words. Dr. Suess won the bet by writing *Green Eggs and Ham*.

70

Better Jewelry, Better Jeweler?

If you had to choose between selling what you wanted to sell, or what the majority of people wanted to buy, which would you choose?

Are you sure? The truth is that you've already chosen, and your success in selling is determined largely by your answer to that question. Are you selling what you want to sell, or what the people want to buy?

Noted counselor Richard Exley warns that we Americans are beginning to define ourselves by our career choices, and not just externally, but internally as well. Many of us define who we are by what we do, and we suffer mentally and emotionally as a result.

Think about it. Does selling a better-quality product help you see yourself as a better-quality person? When you sell an important customer, does it make you feel more important?

It's certainly not my intention to preach at you, but this is a matter that relates directly to advertising and marketing. I think you'll see my point in a moment.

The sales volume of a retailer will be determined solely by the retailer's ability to serve the public in the manner the public best likes to be served.

The retailer often says to advertising, "Here's what I want to sell. Now you go make people want to buy it," never stopping to consider how much easier it would be if he would simply sell what the public wants to buy.

This whole issue came to light recently in a staff meeting. We were searching for the common characteristics of clients who were experiencing rampant success when one of my associates said, "Have you

See ch. 14, "The Changing Face of the Rich."

ever noticed that the client who has an axe to grind never seems to do as well as the client who just wants everyone to be happy?"

A willingness to do what it takes to be successful won't make you a dishonest person. What it will do is make you sensitive to what people want, and much more willing to give it to them. Increased sales and higher volume will be your just reward.

It's the American Way.

If it is not in the interest of the public, it is not in the interest of business.

Joseph H. DeFrees

71

Waiting for Breakthrough

What would be your opinion of a farmer who plants an apple seed, then returns a few days later and says, "This ain't working. I must have planted this seed in the wrong soil"? That's exactly how most advertisers handle their advertising. Expecting a quick payoff, these businesspeople plant only those seeds that develop most quickly but must be planted again and again and again. The seeds they most often plant are ads that make a limited-time offer and, in so doing, create an artificial sense of urgency.

When it comes to understanding breakthrough, farmers are smarter than the rest of us. They know they must wait until the seed has grown to maturity before the crop is ready to harvest. That's just how the universe works.

Understanding the law of seedtime and harvest, the farmer is prepared to toil and wait patiently for breakthrough, the magical moment that will justify his investment of time and energy. He faithfully tends fields that show no visible sign of seeds growing beneath the soil, because he has complete confidence in the immutable laws of the universe.

The farmer knows that any crop that matures quickly is one that will have to be planted again and again. Should the farmer choose to invest his energies in a recurring crop, such as grapes, apples, or cherries, he knows that such crops take much longer to mature before they ever bear any fruit. But he also knows that he can plan on reaping a lifetime of harvests from a single planting.

Why can't businesspeople get this through their heads? Demanding instant gratification, the typical advertiser plants only the crops that develop most quickly, the ones that must be planted again and again. The seeds he plants most often are ads that make a limited-time offer and create an artificial sense of urgency. But when the sale ends — "Saturday night at nine" — so does all the benefit from the ads. The advertiser must then go back to the beginning and start all over again.

Most businesspeople advertise badly because they lack faith in the law of seedtime and harvest. They won't believe that the seed of their message is growing beneath the soil of the mind when there is no visible evidence of it. The self-inflicted punishment for this lack of faith will be a lifetime of promotions, special events, and discount hype as they frantically plant one short-term crop after another.

Don't fall into the trap of artificial urgency. Get in step with the law of seedtime and harvest. Invest your energy in long-term advertising. Say things the customer is sure to remember when she has need of your product or service. Don't put an "expiration date" on your message. In the beginning, you'll need a great deal of faith and patience, but when breakthrough finally arrives, you'll harvest a bigger and richer crop with every passing year.

The only thing you'll need then is a good banker.

**As long as the earth endures,
seedtime and harvest . . .
will never cease.**

God's promise to Noah, Genesis 8:22

72

The Other Side of Breakthrough

When a jet breaks the sound barrier, the air can't get out of its way fast enough, and you hear a terrific "Boom!" The sign of your business reaching breakthrough is equally dramatic: your company instantly outgrows its bank account. All at once you need to accumulate more inventory, hire more people, and add more square footage than you can fund from current profits.

As odd as this may sound, having too much business can be far more dangerous than having too little. An enormous percentage of the bankruptcies that happen each year are simply the result of businesses outgrowing their operating capital and borrowing power.

Clay Cary, vice president of the lending division at Frost Bank in Austin, says, "Few business owners understand the perspective of the person they are trying to persuade to loan them money. Even more rarely do business owners understand all the ramifications of rapid growth, and consequently they have a hard time saying no to new sales opportunities. Yet if they're not properly capitalized or don't have sufficient borrowing lined up, it's usually better to turn business away than to let that next sale drive them to the poor house."

Farmers deal with breakthrough as a matter of course. They know that seeds of a single species planted in the same field at the same time will germinate and grow at about the same rate. When the average plant has grown to maturity, the entire crop is ready for harvest. And that's when the real work begins — bringing in the harvest before the crop spoils.

If your message has its intended effect, you may generate more business than you can handle. Do you have enough cash on hand to order the merchandise you will need to satisfy the demand? Do you

See ch. 66, "Banker Talk."

158

have the room to accommodate the goods and people that will come your way? Do you have the staff to handle customers' needs and requests? If not, you'll not only fail to benefit from the opportunities you've created with your advertising, you'll be sending away large numbers of unhappy people who will think twice before darkening your door again.

On the other hand, if you've managed to borrow enough money to prepare for the expected wave of business, have you arranged to pay off your loans comfortably if your sales don't quite meet your goals? Will you end up paying to store large inventories that aren't bringing in the cash you owe to your hard-nosed banker? Can you pay the people you've hired to help you, people who are depending on you for their living?

Your ads are out there working for you, growing in the fertile minds of future customers. Are you ready for the harvest?

The only things that evolve by themselves
in an organization are disorder, friction,
and malperformance.

Peter Drucker

73

Huebner's Sixth Rule of Mountaineering:
There's Always Room on the Rope
for a Person with Honor

Huebner's sixth rule instantly reminds me of a statement made by Gary Wortman: "When you meet the right person, hire him. Don't worry about whether you have a position available or the budget for it. Always make room for a good employee."

I've followed Gary's advice for the past ten years and have never once regretted it. A great person pulls everyone around him upward, and when an entire team is doing it together, the result can be truly amazing. With every new addition to our staff, the bar is raised, and a new standard of excellence results from it. (I feel lucky to own the company because I'm no longer sure I could get a job here if I didn't.)

Huebner's Six Rules
of Mountaineering:
See pp. 37–38.

If you want employees to do a <u>good</u> job, tell them what you <u>want</u> and encourage them to succeed. If you want employees to do a <u>great</u> job, tell them what you <u>need</u> and give them permission to fail.

Richard Kessler

This is the last photograph of George Leigh Mallory and Andrew Irvine, taken as they prepared for their final attempt to reach the summit of Mt. Everest. They disappeared June 8, 1924 and were never seen alive again. Mallory's body was recently found at 27,000 feet.

74

Mountain-Climbing Millionaires

Not yet thirty, Billie is a self-made millionaire. He doesn't drink, smoke, or dance, and he gives lavishly to politicians. Everyone wants Billie's opinion. Even the president of the United States solicits Billie's advice. Billie is on top of the world. He's made it to the peak of the mountain. It doesn't get any better than this.

In accepting his award from the U.S. Junior Chamber of Commerce as one of America's Outstanding Young Men, Billie says, "I owe my success to clean living." When the awards ceremony is over, Billie chuckles to a friend, "They'll never catch up with me. These people are stupid."

With a firm handshake and a winning smile, Billie romances wealthy private investors and secures massive government funding for more than 33,000 rural fertilizer storage tanks. He then purchases a few hundred tanks and scatters them around West Texas. Tens of millions of dollars go into Billie's pocket.

When a friend asks Billie where he got the inspiration for his scheme, Billie explains how Texas ranchers have long borrowed heavily from the bank, putting up their cattle for collateral, then driven the bankers around on vast tracts of land to get a general count of the livestock. "Those bankers never realize they're counting the same cattle over and over again from different vantage points on the ranch," says Billie. "It'll be the same way with my storage tanks. I'll starve them to death looking for equipment."

When he was young, Billie Sol Estes had a plan for getting rich quick and it worked. He made it to the top of the mountain. Now in his seventies, Billie has spent most of his adult life in prison because he was a brilliant schemer who told himself, "Time is the enemy.

Hard work is for others. Cleverness is the key to success." Billie refused to believe the mountain climbers who said, "Time is your ally. Hard work is inevitable. Persistence is the key to success. The best way to climb a mountain is to take one small step after another."

Which of these ideologies best describes your beliefs? Do you consider time to be your enemy or your friend? Is hard work a thing to be escaped or embraced? Do you depend more on your cleverness or your persistence? It seems to me the American public is equally divided on these issues. Having considered the matter at length, I'm convinced that at least half of us are schemers at heart.

Don't get me wrong. Scheming doesn't always involve illegal activities. It's more about a belief system that says, "Time is the enemy. Hard work is for others. Cleverness is the key to success." Schemers believe they can build real estate empires "with nothing down," and that multilevel marketing is the fast track to the good life. Schemers aren't necessarily bad people. I'd say at least half of my closest friends are schemers, and I very much enjoy their companionship.

I just don't let them carry my wallet.

There is no royal road to anything.
One thing at a time,
and all things in succession.
That which grows slowly endures.

Josiah G. Holland

75

A Bright Red Bow Tie

fter speaking to a local business club, I walk into our home and say, "Pennie, I met the most delightful old man today."

"Oh really?" she answers. "What made him special?"

I think for a moment, then answer, "Well, before I began speaking, all of the hundred or so people in the audience stood up, one at a time, to introduce themselves." Knowing how I feel about tedious formalities, Pennie smiles as I continue, "I'm about to fall asleep when this colorful gentleman bounces to his feet and begins to introduce his young guest in such a way as to make me feel honored to be in the same room with the kid! In less than sixty seconds, this magnetic fellow had the whole room believing that his young guest was about the most talented person on earth! The unfortunate thing was that the old guy never got around to introducing himself — just his guest. I really wish I knew who he was, because I'd like to get to know him."

Pennie looks thoughtful for a moment. She asks, "Was he wearing a bright red bow tie?"

"Why, yes!" I answer, "How did you know?"

When she finally finishes laughing, she says, "Honey, I really wish you'd read the newspaper once in a while. You're probably the only person in the state who wouldn't recognize Willie Kocurek."

Confused, I ask, "Other than a really delightful character, who the heck is Willie Kocurek?"

Pennie walks briefly out of the room and returns with a newspaper in hand. "Last month," she says, "Willie and Maureen appeared on *Good Morning America,* and just two days ago the newspaper ran a front-page story about his appearance at the elementary school that's named after him. There's hardly a month that goes by that Willie Kocurek isn't featured in a major story. Honey, the man is a legend."

Now armed with a name, I get Mr. Kocurek on the phone and learn that he spent most of his business life running a mom 'n' pop appliance store that was famous for its homemade ads.

"All my newspaper ads looked like they were hand-drawn by a three-year-old child," he says. "If there had been two of us with ads like that, then both of us would've had bad ads. But since mine were the only ones like that, they absolutely worked miracles." And in every single ad he wrote, whether for newspaper or radio or television, Willie would always promise his customers, "You don't need money, just a little-bit-a-month," and he always wrapped up by saying, "Where there's a Willie, there's a way."

When Willie left the appliance business at the age of sixty-seven, he entered law school because he "didn't want to be tired or *re*-tired." Willie showed up for class each and every day in a red bow tie just like the ones he's worn every day of his life since FDR was president. At age seventy, he got his law degree. Today Willie Kocurek is eighty-eight years old and still practicing the law with vigor.

Having spent some time pondering my new friend Willie, I've come to the conclusion that the success of Colonel Harland Sanders had very little to do with his eleven secret herbs and spices. The Colonel's real secrets were his unmitigated audacity and his extraordinary confidence. How many people do you know with the nerve to dress like that? The man wore a white, double-breasted suit with a goofy black string tie and carried a black enamel cane, for gosh sake! Yet no one ever accused the Colonel of looking silly. Harland Sanders wore that suit with such quiet confidence that no one ever thought him to be dressed strangely at all.

Unmitigated audacity and extraordinary confidence are the special domain of only two kinds of people: the amazingly successful and

See ch. 7, "What Is Branding?" and ch. 15, "Out of Style."

See ch. 46, "Huebner's Second Rule of Mountaineering: No Guts, No Glory."

the extremely deranged. Colonel Sanders was not deranged. Neither is Willie Kocurek.

How much do you believe in you? Do you have the courage to go your own direction? Are you the kind of person who could wear a red bow tie with confidence?

76

Writing Classified Ads for Employment

Austin-based ad firm seeks gopher for odd jobs and small projects. Mail room work. Some lifting required. Must be reliable and have own car. $1,500/mo.

hat's this ad really saying? To the prospective employee, it speaks of limited opportunity and meaningless work. It firmly necessitates that the prospect be nothing more than an uncreative widget mover without ambition — a dolt. In all probability, the ad will attract those who are suitable only for odd jobs and small projects. Is that the employee you're looking for? Or would you rather have this one?

Entry Level Opportunity of a Lifetime: Are you dependable and resourceful? Do you have lots of energy, intuition, and initiative? Do you dress well, have computer skills? Are you willing to pick up clients at the airport, wash dishes, vacuum carpets, conduct telephone surveys, run errands, and do all the other things we don't have time to do? We are an advertising firm with clients nationwide and we need a super-gopher. No whiners. No lazy people. Nobody with too many "personal commitments." South Austin. $1,500/mo.

Now, what is *this* ad really saying? To me, it said everything. A week out of college, I saw my future in this ad. Though the ad clearly denoted the grunt work involved in the job, it did so in the form of a challenging question: Can you handle it, punk? Hell, yes, I said. Especially if it meant I could be energetic and intuitive and use my initiative at the entry-level opportunity of a lifetime working for an advertising firm. I'm no whiner, I'm not lazy, I said. I couldn't wait to

See ch. 62, "Huebner's First Rule of Mountaineering: Climb with Passion."

call. I was, most certainly, their man. As it turns out, more than 220 other applicants thought I was wrong — but I beat 'em all!

When the Wizard wrote that ad three years ago, he was looking for a super-gopher. I think he got one. But he also got a writer who is now the head of his Message Development Department. The Wizard found his man by being liberal with his words, by asking questions that would resonate in the heart of a specific person, by giving life and hope to a job that could easily have blended in with all the other classifieds that were dulled by their lack of respect for the position. The ad was so effective that it has become the template from which we write classified ads for all our clients.

Chris Maddock

Yes, This is the same Chris you read about in chapter 66 of The Wizard of Ads.

See ch. 36, "Intellect vs. Emotion."

Writing Classified Ads for Employment

Rule 1. The ad should be about the employee, not the job. Right now, someone is perusing the classifieds who is perfect for the position you hope to fill. If only you could figure out how to motivate him. Like you and me, this person has aspirations, interests, and strengths. So how do you make your ad more compelling than the others? What is the magic ingredient that will make your ad irresistible? You need only describe the person you hope to find! Speak to his aspirations, interests, and strengths. Your dream employee will probably not know of your business. He will not recognize the job you detail. You can, however, be confident that he will recognize himself when that is who you describe. He will see himself in the words you choose, the actions you prescribe, and the admirable traits you require. "That's me!" he will cry. "What a perfect fit! Honey, where's the phone? 'Cause today is the start of the rest of my life!"

Rule 2. Questions are the answer. There's nothing more irresistible than a question. Have you ever tried to ignore one? Have you ever read a question that was aimed at you and completely escaped thinking about the answer? I doubt it. If, in your classified ads, you are willing to ask for exactly what you want, you will probably get it. By raising the bar and challenging a prospect to answer your questions, you will weed out the losers and energize the winners.

"Do you believe the best is yet to come?"

"Are you willing to take risks?"

"Can you make a difference in our company?"

See ch. 73, "Huebner's Sixth Rule of Mountaineering: There's Always Room on the Rope for a Person with Honor."

When your future employee reads a description of herself in your ad, she will feel like she's looking into a mirror. "Wow!" she will think. "What serendipity! This is the position I was born to fill!"

Rule 3. You get what you pay for. You already know that the cheapest option is rarely the best. In fact, life has probably taught you that when something really matters, the best thing to do is to spend a little extra. This is certainly true for classified ads. Stingy, short, choppy ads communicate a lack of respect for the position. They give the impression that you really don't care. They effectively say, "Take it or leave it."

Most will leave it.

Classifieds ads are no different than ads that sell a product or service. If you want a classified ad to be boring, write about the job. If you want it to work miracles, write about the person you hope to find, and don't be stingy with your words.

It is a fine thing to have ability, but the ability to discover ability in others is the true test.

Elbert Hubbard

CEO WANTED

Tall, homely man needed for four years to guide growing nation through desperate political and military straits. Must be able to recruit and military straits to give their lives for the Union; organize, supply, and lead armies; balance competing interests; hire brilliant diplomatic fire insubordinate subordinates; oversee development of national frontiers; and solve a multitude of frustrating national problems as they occur. No experience necessary, no references required. Send vitae and SASE to Govt Of By & For People, PO Drawer X, Washington, D.C.

DISHWASHERS

Positions available for persons with experience scraping dishes, soaking dishes, stacking dishes, scrubbing

77

Right Person, Wrong Job

S teve, I've been meaning to tell you how much I admire your ability to make people feel at ease. There have been several times that I've seen you step in and help resolve disputes between your co-workers, and I want you to know how much I appreciate that. Your talents as a peacemaker are a valuable part of your skill package, and I'm convinced that we're probably underutilizing those skills in your current position. Frankly, I've often thought you could have a brilliant future as an arbitrator if you ever chose to go that direction, and I've occasionally wondered why you've never pursued it.

"I also appreciate the fact that you're the first one here each morning and that you never complain about the long hours. I wish all my employees had your attitude.

"The problem I'm facing today is that your current job description requires a skill package that's considerably different from yours, even though I consider you to be a highly skilled and extremely valuable employee. I feel like I've got the right person, but in the wrong job, and there's just not a position in the company that fits your skills right now.

"Steve, I'm convinced that you've got a bright future, but this company isn't the right place for you. Even though it may not feel like it today, some day you're going to thank me for forcing you to find the wonderful job that I'm certain is out there waiting for you. (Handing envelope across the desk.) I've prepared a glowing letter of recommendation and enclosed it with your final paycheck. I'm convinced that any company with a job opening that requires a person of your skills is going to call and thank me for making you available.

(Now standing up with hand outstretched for a final handshake.) Some day, I believe you'll thank me, too."

Firing with compassion is easier on the employee and it's easier on you. The only thing less pleasant than being the boss who has to fire an employee is being the employee fired by a boss who needs to feel justified in letting you go. How might Steve have felt if his boss had dismissed him in the traditional way? "Steve, this is the third month in a row you've missed your sales goal. Frankly, I believe you could have made those goals if you hadn't spent so much time sticking your nose where it didn't belong. Sometimes I think you're more interested in making sure everyone likes you than in doing your job. You blew the Kowalski deal and you dropped the ball on the McMasters account. You just don't have the eye of the tiger, boy. You don't have the killer instinct. I'm afraid I'm gonna have to let you go. You've been a real disappointment. Here's your final paycheck. Clean out your desk."

Few days in life feel as bleak as the day one is fired from a job. Why make a difficult time harder than it has to be? Even the worst employee has a few positive traits you can highlight during the termination. Why not let him leave with his dignity intact? Why not let him feel okay about having been "the right person in the wrong job"? It certainly makes it easier for the employee to go home and tell the family what's happened, and it doesn't cost you a dime.

See ch. 99, "Huebner's Fourth Rule of Mountaineering: Never Turn Your Back on Your Partner."

Latent abilities are like clay. It can be mud on shoes, brick in a building, or a statue that will inspire all who see it. The clay is the same. The result is dependent on how it is used.

James F. Lincoln

78

Regression to the Mean

Sometimes I think my CD player has a mind of its own. Randomly accessing a library of more than 1,400 songs contained on 100 compact discs, the player occasionally enters a stream of consciousness in which it plays all my favorites in such skillful arrangement that I find myself thinking I should drop a ten-dollar bill in its tip jar. Then I remember, it's only an electronic appliance. About that time the machine will go into such a long series of losers that I finally turn the darn thing off. In reality, the machine is simple proof of the mathematic principle of regression to the mean.

An arithmetic term, "mean" was defined in 1767 as "a value that is computed by dividing the sum of a set of terms by the number of terms." In 1947 we revised the definition to be "the sum of the values of a random variable with each value multiplied by its probability of occurrence, or the integral of the product of a probability density function of a continuous random variable and the random variable itself when taken over all possible values of the variable."

If you ask me, the mean is just a middle point between extremes.

Not being a mathematician myself, I owe my understanding of "regression to the mean" to Professors Kahneman and Tversky (see chapter 40), partners who experienced an epiphany while trying to convince a group of Top Gun pilot instructors of the intrinsic value of praise. When Kahneman and Tversky told the instructors that their students would respond faster to praise than to ridicule, the instructors were unanimously adamant in their ferocity against the advice. "We've tried that crap and it doesn't work!" they shouted. "Any time

a student makes a perfect three-point landing and is praised for it, you can bet the next landing will be worse. But if the same student makes a horrible landing and you yell at him for it, the next one will usually be better."

It was precisely then that the light bulb appeared over Tversky's head. "Gentlemen, what you've been witnessing has nothing to do with your reinforcement, either positive or negative. What you're seeing is merely regression to the mean. When a student makes a perfect landing, it's nearly certain that the next one will be worse, regardless of whether the student is praised or punished. Likewise, a horrible landing will almost always be followed by a better one, no matter what you do. What we're trying to teach you is how to more quickly raise the quality of the *average* landing."

Clients never demand explanations from me when they're having an unusually good month, but they always want me to give them a detailed explanation any time their business begins to slow down. They want to know why things have changed, and they expect me to be able to tell them exactly what the slowdown means.

Sometimes it means a competitor has begun taking a bigger bite of the pie. Sometimes it means the client's sales staff has begun dropping the ball internally. Sometimes it means the weather has got everyone acting silly. Sometimes it doesn't mean anything at all, it's just regression to the mean, a sort of payback for the previous month when things were unusually good (though no one is ever willing to consider this as an explanation).

Maybe I should lend them my CD player. . . .

79

How to Get Exceptional Service

Have you ever noticed how the smallest and most petty people are the quickest to demand their "rights"? Day after day, I see pompous, self-important people make outrageous and high-toned demands upon cashiers, ticket agents, and waitresses across America, in effect saying, "I demand my rights."

Every time I see this happen, I want to interrupt and say, "Upon what, exactly, are these rights based, and who, exactly, enforces them for you? In demanding your rights, aren't you really just imposing your stronger will on the weaker will of another? Aren't you simply abusing a person who has a greater sense of etiquette than your own? Is fear the only motivator you know how to use?"

I'm always entertained by watching these same excitable little people when they feel they have a gun to my head. Having little fear and virtually no etiquette, my instant response is to say, "Okay, big boy, let's hear the gun go Boom. I want you to go ahead and do all these bad things you threaten. I promise you my undivided attention, but it's time to get started. Now let the show begin." I have never yet met a person who really had a gun or was ready to pull the trigger. One after the other, they grow angrily confused and then walk away in frustration like so many Barney Fifes and George Costanzas.

Is extraordinary service from the waitress all you want? It's really not that hard to get! All you have to do is glance at her name tag and then say her name with a smile every time she speaks to you. "Yes, Kathy, I'd love some more coffee, thanks." It's amazing how often people will respond like friends when you treat them like friends.

Make an experiment of it. Seriously. Watch for name tags this week and take advantage of every opportunity to call others by name.

I believe you will be both startled and saddened by what you learn. Startled, because of the universally positive reactions you will see; saddened, when you realize that no one else is doing it.

You have the right to make others feel valuable, important, and loved. Oddly enough, it's a right you will never have to demand.

In the business of life, Man is the only product. And there is only one direction in which man can possibly develop if he is to make a better living or yield a bigger dividend to himself, to his race, to nature or to God. He must grow in knowledge, wisdom, kindliness and understanding.

V. C. Kitchen

80

Would You Believe
Twenty-Six to One?

An in-depth study conducted by Technical Assistance Research Programs of Washington, D.C., uncovered some things I think you should know:

1. On average, twenty-six unhappy customers won't complain for every one who will.

2. Yet each of these twenty-seven unhappy customers will tell an average of sixteen other people about his bad experience with your firm.

3. This means every complaint you hear represents 432 negative impressions.

How many people should have to complain to you before you take action to permanently remedy a problem? By the time you hear a particular complaint three times, the problem has been mentioned to an average of 1,296 people.

4. It costs five times as much to attract a new customer as it costs to keep an old one.

5. Ninety-one percent of your unhappy customers will never buy from you again.

6. But if you make a focused effort to remedy your customers' complaints, 82 percent of them will stay with you.

What should you do when people complain? Above all, don't become defensive! You need to communicate with an attitude that says, "I want to understand the problem so I can fix it and make you happy." Here are three questions to ask that will bail you out every time:

1. "What has happened?" Ask this question calmly and with genuine concern.

See "word-of-mouth advertising," p. 128.

2. "What should have happened?" You must clearly understand the customer's expectations before you can attempt to correct the problem.

3. "What can I do to make it right?" This will calm even the angriest customer.

Now go find an unhappy customer and turn his day around.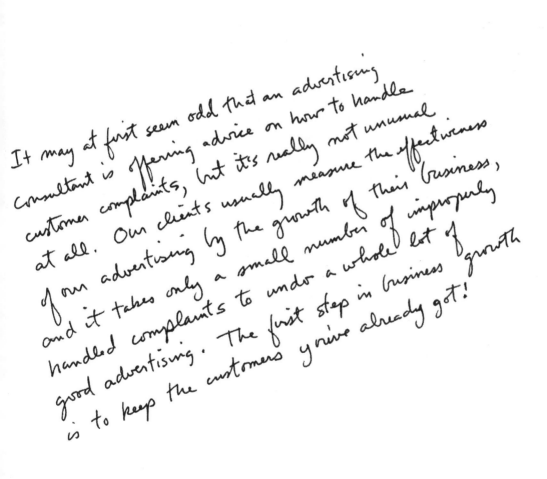

It may at first seem odd that an advertising consultant is offering advice on how to handle customer complaints, but it's really not unusual at all. Our clients usually measure the effectiveness of our advertising by the growth of their business, and it takes only a small number of improperly handled complaints to undo a whole lot of good advertising. The first step in business growth is to keep the customers you've already got!

81

Huebner's Third Rule of Mountaineering: Expect Dead Ends

There will be times when you come to a fork in the road and, after much deliberation, choose the wrong way. A great deal of time and money will be lost before you can correct your mistake. Get over it.

The secret of strategic planning is to budget both time and money for dealing with the truly unexpected, so that when it happens, your plan doesn't fall apart. (When driving to the airport to catch a flight, we always allow an additional fifteen minutes for a traffic jam. We have no way of knowing where it will be, only that there's likely to be one.)

Huebner's Six Rules of Mountaineering: See pp. 37–38.

International business consultants Fox and Mancuso advise their clients, "In calculating rough costs for a product made overseas, add 20 percent to the cost of the product when it leaves the plant, wherever that is." Notice that Fox and Mancuso don't pretend to know exactly why the extra money will have to be spent, only that it will. Do you take "dead ends" into consideration in your planning, or are you planning to do business in a dream world?

It's impossible to forecast when problems will arise, but it's fairly certain that they will. Are you mentally prepared for them? Do you have the tenacity to persevere, or will you panic and throw your hands into the air, crying, "I didn't plan on this!"?

Let's learn and label properly Disappointment and Discouragement for what they are — two completely different states of mind. Disappointment can be a spur to improvement that will contribute to success. But Discouragement is a mortal enemy that destroys courage and robs one of the will to fight. It is not circumstance that causes Discouragement, but one's own reaction to that circumstance. Everyone must meet Disappointment, many times; it is simply a part of life. When it is met, we may resign ourselves to Discouragement and failure. Or we may recognize each Disappointment as an asset by which we can profit, and take new strength from a lesson learned. The choice is ours, each time, to make.

John M. Wilson

82

Don't Get Your Panties in a Bind

Acquaintances with important degrees from important universities are often outraged when they learn how much I charge for the benefit of my private observations. When I cheerfully and openly admit to these friends that I do, indeed, fabricate all that I know, or think I know, from the raw material of my own experience, it always puts their panties in a bind. (In other words, it makes them extremely uncomfortable.)

My educated friends don't feel it's right, somehow, that a person should be able to sell what he has learned when the method of his learning has been unsupervised listening and watching and reading and asking. They feel that I should be poor.

I'm telling you this because I'm about to share with you a controversial observation that might possibly be wrong, though I am unconditionally convinced of the truth of it. (If you disagree with me, please don't let it twist your trousers.)

I believe that most businesspeople are unnecessarily preoccupied with the future. These businesspeople see the world changing at a precipitous rate and consequently assume they must correctly forecast the future if they hope to find any success there.

I completely disagree.

No one will ever be able to forecast the events of tomorrow. Prognosticators of the future are wrong far more often than they are right. If you and I are to prepare for the future, I believe we must study the past. (Those shorts still okay?)

The simple truth is that we are not making new mistakes. We are making the old mistakes over and over again. Most of us will probably continue to make the old mistakes far into the future.

I believe we are attracted to the future like moths to a flame because the future is titillating. Exciting. Unknowable. Fantastic. And the boring past can always be viewed with 20/20 hindsight.

But that's the magic of it.

If you study and learn from the recurrent mistakes humankind has made through the centuries, and if you study the recurrent elements of our greatest successes, then you will be prepared for the future, regardless of what tomorrow may bring.

Failure is success if we learn from it.

Malcolm Forbes

83

Of All the Bad Luck!

Dean Rhoads met Dave Thomas long before Dave ever opened his first Wendy's Hamburgers location. "Fort Wayne wasn't a large town in those days, so when I needed an extra hand, I'd often call on young Dave to help me out. It's a great pity for me that I didn't invest in Wendy's," says Dean, "because I really liked that boy and I always knew that he would someday do something big."

Strike one.

Dave worked at the local Kentucky Fried Chicken location, one of the Colonel's first. "I met Colonel Sanders," says Dean, "and I had opportunity to buy stock in his company early on, but I didn't agree with some of his ideas, so I didn't invest in it."

Strike two.

Like Dave Thomas and Colonel Sanders, Dean was also something of a pioneer in food service. It was his company, Lincoln Manufacturing, that perfected the first system for keeping food hot while it was waiting to be served. "Despite everything I tried, I could not succeed; I was barely making payroll. I remember many an evening pacing the floor in my office, trying to think through what I was doing.

"Since I was in the restaurant equipment business, it wasn't uncommon for me to have several equipment salesmen in my waiting room, each one hoping to be able to meet me and sell me something. One of these fellows, Ray was his name, sold a gadget called a multi-mixer that could mix five milkshakes at a time. He was very pleasant, but didn't appear to me to have any unusual or outstanding characteristics that would inspire me to invest in his new venture, so when I heard that Ray had bought a little hamburger stand called McDonald's, I chose not to invest."

Strike three.

"Ultimately, my Lincoln system of food service was adopted by schools and institutions throughout the USA and a whole new industry was born. Finally I could afford to take a much-needed vacation, so I decided to go on a cruise. During the cruise, I met an attorney from the Pacific Northwest who told really funny stories about how his son Billy and his friends would sit at the kitchen table and try to make useful gadgets from baskets of electronic components. He told me that his son was really bright and that I should consider investing in his new company. I thought, 'What kind of kid would name a company Microsoft? What's soft about an electronic gadget?' So I didn't invest."

Wait a minute, wasn't Dean supposed to leave the batter's box after the third strike?

Right now you're thinking Dean Rhoads probably spends most of his time telling sad stories about what might have been, right? Well nothing could be further from the truth. You see, Dean pursued his own vision, investing everything he had in himself and his dream until the day he saw his name at number 289 on the Forbes list of the 400 most successful business owners in America. The little company that "could barely make payroll" was now doing more than $410 million in annual volume. (Later it did $689 million.)

See ch. 81, "Huebner's Third Rule of Mountaineering: Expect Dead Ends."

In the game of life, there's no rule that says you have to leave the batter's box after your third strike. If you're smart, you'll do like Dean and just keep on swingin' till you finally hit a grand slam. The game's not over till you walk away from the plate.

Giving up is the ultimate tragedy.

Robert J. Donovan

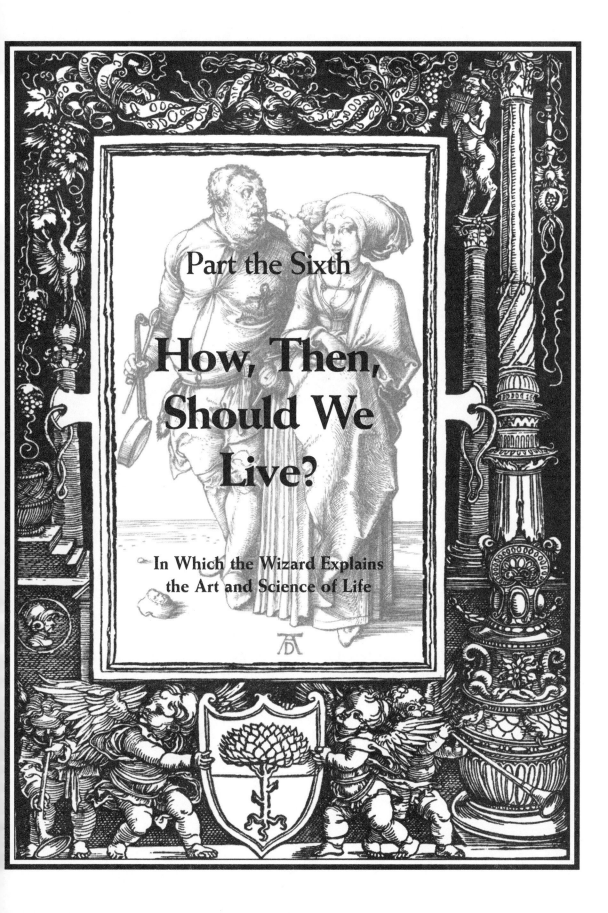

Part the Sixth

How, Then, Should We Live?

In Which the Wizard Explains the Art and Science of Life

84

The American Year

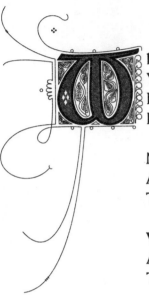

White Wind is duty, pure and clean.
Yellow Fire has high and lofty dreams.
Red Earth is all adventure, Tom Sawyer to the core.
Blue Rain is quiet wisdom. Who could ask for more?

North, South, East, West:
Arrows pointing in four directions;
The compass that brought us here.

Winter, Spring, Summer, Fall:
A quartet singing in harmony;
The four faces of our year.

George, Tom, Teddy, Abe:
A mirror in shining Dakota granite,
Reflecting what we hope to gain.

Washington, Jefferson, Roosevelt, Lincoln:
White Wind, Yellow Fire, Red Earth, Blue Rain.

(Yes, I'm in one of those strange moods that makes people sometimes wonder if I have a ponytail and play guitar. . . . The answers, by the way, are "No" and "No.")

This poem comes from my recent realization that the soul of America is perfectly revealed in the faces on Mt. Rushmore.

George Washington was a man driven by obligation and sacrifice, the perfect symbol of every father who ever marched off to war.

Thomas Jefferson was a visionary of high ideals who saw in his heart what America ought to be, but in his flesh fell short of it. He wrote, "All men are created equal," and inspired hundreds of his countrymen to free their slaves, yet Jefferson never freed his own. The author of the document that made us a nation, Thomas Jefferson lived a life of quiet hypocrisy. But I'm reluctant to cast the first stone. How often have I failed to live up to the standards I believe in?

Teddy Roosevelt was rambunctious in his boyish enthusiasm, as much a maverick and a renegade as any hippie who ever burned a draft card.

Abraham Lincoln was physically ugly, but he held us together with the wisdom and tenacious commitment of a mother watching over her children — the embodiment of American grit and determination.

No single one of these figures is capable of telling the American story alone, yet together they sing it in perfect harmony. Four faces on a mountainside: the four seasons of the American year. 🐾

85

Will You Go for the High Note?

In one of his inquisitive moods, my friend Eric Rhoads recently asked Joan Rivers, "Why does one performer become a living legend while other performers fade off the scene? What, exactly, is the difference between a star and a superstar?" Like most of Eric's questions, this one seemed unanswerable to me. But then I'm not Joan Rivers.

"Eric, that's easy," said Joan, "Most stars play it safe because they have too much to lose. Superstars are the ones who throw caution to the wind; improvise impulsively; go for the high note. Superstars give it everything they've got and hold back nothing at all. In a word," said Joan, "the difference is guts."

I'm convinced Joan Rivers was right. How many times have we seen the favored ice skater come in second because she "played it safe" and did the double toe loop instead of going for the triple? How many times have we seen a basketball team give up an insurmountable lead when they attempted to play it safe and tried to stall? How many times has a football team lost the game by retreating into a "prevent" defense? It appears to me that playing it safe is about the least safe thing you can do!

In our office, when someone has been acting fearful or small, standard procedure is to show him a forefinger and thumb held about a half-inch apart. I've never been exactly sure what this gesture means, but it seems to say, "Go for the high note. Don't be a weasel. Attempt the triple toe loop."

Does everyone who attempts the triple toe loop come from behind to win the gold medal? Nope. Sometimes they land in a heap on the

See ch. 46, "Huebner's Second Rule of Mountaineering: No Guts, No Glory."

ice. So what will it be? Will you go for the gold, or should I hold my forefinger and thumb half an inch apart as I look into your eyes?

The auditorium is dark. The audience is waiting. The spotlight awaits your arrival. What are you going to do?

Undertake something that is difficult; it will do you good. Unless you try to do something beyond what you have already mastered, you will never grow.

Ronald E. Osborn

86

George Just Wants to Be Left Alone

George has been without a Daddy since he was ten years old. A quiet boy, George mostly likes to put seeds in the ground and then watch over them as they sprout and grow. He doesn't get to do this very often, though, because people are always taking advantage of George's highly developed sense of duty. George mostly just wants to be left alone, but the people around him don't seem to care what George wants. Duty is George's undoing.

As a young man, George is involved in a protest against the government, and his highly patriotic mother never forgives him. She complains bitterly about her "unpatriotic son" until the day she dies. "Oh, well," thinks George, "no one is perfect."

"Dutiful George" becomes widely known for quietly accomplishing whatever is asked of him, and in later years he wonders whether this might have been his biggest mistake. "No matter how much I do," thinks George, "people always want me to do more. I never get to put seeds in the ground anymore, and even if I did, no one would give me the time to watch them sprout and grow." George sometimes wonders whether things would have turned out differently if he had just learned to say, "No. You'll have to find someone else."

But George continues to do whatever is asked of him, and when he is sixty-four, he surprises his employers by delivering a heartfelt speech in which he begs them to let him retire. His bosses keep George on the job for another three years, but late one autumn afternoon, George is finally given the freedom to return to his fields.

Day after day, George spends his retirement in quiet anticipation of springtime, thinking of seeds and soil and sunshine and of having plenty of time to watch things sprout and grow. Sadly, George dies that winter, having never had the chance to grow anything but a baby nation.

But we Americans are not an ungrateful people, so we print George's face on our dollar bills and celebrate his birthday each February. And I, for one, quietly hope that George found some small satisfaction in planting the seeds of a nation and then watching that nation sprout and grow. I like to believe that if George had it all to do over again, he would make the same choices and do the same things.

How about you? Are you irritated that you are being asked to do your duty? Do you resent the fact that no one seems to be willing to let you do what you really want? Have you been asked to subordinate your private desires to a greater good? If so, take a lesson from George and try to make the best of your situation. Maybe it will turn out all right in the end.

A man searches the world over for what he needs, and then returns home to find it.

George Moore

87

Poky's Wisdom

He just pokes along and looks at the trees. He looks at the flowers and he looks at the bees. With a smile on his face he says, "Haste makes waste. You've got to stop, look, and learn as you go!" That's the Poky Little Puppy, and he's the smartest little puppy I know. (Barkbarkbarkbark!)

I haven't listened to that little song or read the book that inspired it for at least thirty-five years, but the story of the Poky Little Puppy has been a guiding influence in my life since I was four years old.

"Stop, look, and learn as you go," seemed like good advice when I was four, so that's essentially all I've done since then. In the ensuing four decades, here's what I've discovered:

1. When you stop and look with the intention of learning, the result is often that you "discover" a thing that has long been known by others. This happened to me recently when I found that my pet theory regarding branding (the implantation of associative memories) had already been discovered, tested, and documented by a German psychologist, Hermann Ebbinghaus, in 1885 — work that Pavlov later used as a basis for his own canine experiments.

2. Sometimes you discover a new thing only to learn later that several other people were making precisely the same discovery at exactly the same time. I attribute this phenomenon to the Theory of Universal Knowledge.

3. Occasionally you stop and look and learn a thing that no one has ever learned before. Then you can triumphantly march around the room singing the Poky Little Puppy song at the top of your lungs.

Poky and I believe that you can learn all you need to know by just looking and asking, "What makes that happen?" I am also

See ch. 7, "What Is Branding?" and ch. 42, "Are You Driving the Dog Crazy?"

convinced that you have been uniquely and wonderfully gifted to do whatever it is that will make you the happiest. So why not do it?

Think it over. How many important things in your life have you simply figured out for yourself? Lots, right? But first you had to stop and look. Yes, I know that life's urgencies are driving you far too fast to "stop and look" anymore. You simply can't find the time, right?

Do it anyway.

No, I'm not saying slow down a little. I'm saying, the next time something catches your eye, hit the brakes, pull over to the side of the road, get out of the car, and take a good look around.

Anyway, that's the theory of the Poky Little Puppy. And he's the smartest little puppy I know.

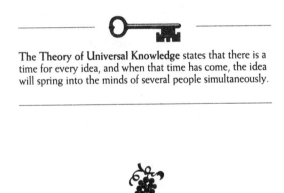

The Theory of Universal Knowledge states that there is a time for every idea, and when that time has come, the idea will spring into the minds of several people simultaneously.

Natural ability without education has more often raised a man to glory and virtue than education without natural ability.

Cicero

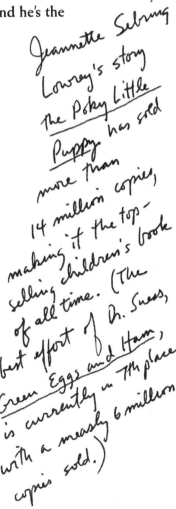

Jeannette Sebring Lowrey's story The Poky Little Puppy has sold more than 14 million copies, making it the top-selling children's book of all time. (The best effort of Dr. Suess, Green Eggs and Ham, is currently in 7th place with a measly 6 million copies sold.)

88

Johnny and Sam

Mason, New Hampshire. Summer, 1788. Thirteen-year-old Johnny Chapman meets young Sam Wilson while visiting his cousin Betsey at her family's farm. Sam and Betsey later marry and move to Troy, New York, where they launch a meat-packing business.

After Sam and Betsey's wedding, Johnny heads west until he comes to a river about nine miles below Steubenville, Ohio. Men describe him as "small, wiry, and restless, with hollow cheeks in a face bronzed by wind and sun and with piercingly brilliant, dark eyes that can surely read the thoughts in a man's soul." He sleeps outdoors, never wearing shoes or carrying weapons. His clothing is a coarse coffee sack with a hole cut in the center for his head, and his only possession is the tin cooking pot he wears like a hat.

For more than fifty years, when settlers arrive to settle a new area they find Chapman already there nursing a small orchard of young apple seedlings. But the man who will be known as Johnny Appleseed doesn't wander the Midwest giving away apple seeds and seedlings. He is a businessman. In Boston, the price of a seedling apple tree is six or seven cents, which is what Johnny charges for his trees out in the wilderness, even though the settlers would gladly pay a great deal more. Throughout his life, Johnny serves his fellow man by preparing apple tree nurseries along the banks of rivers and streams, staying just ahead of the settlers as they move ever westward.

Years pass and Johnny becomes accidentally rich. The wilderness plots on which he planted apple seedlings now mark the center of town after town. He happily sells the land, but uses the money for charity rather than for his own personal comfort. His amazing generosity, startling endurance, and personal faith in God inspire and change a fledgling nation during her most formative years. His name continues to live in legend nearly a century and a half after his passing.

But what of Sam and Betsey?

During the War of 1812, while Johnny is planting apple trees across Ohio and Indiana, Sam and Betsey are supplying the American army with beef in Troy, New York. America is not often referred to as the "United States" during these years, so when Sam marks barrels of army meat with a big "U.S.," not everyone is sure what it means. When a federal inspector asks a watchman why "U.S." is marked on the barrels, the watchman makes a guess: "I think it means Uncle Sam."

Forty years later, the *New York Lantern* publishes the first drawing of "Uncle Sam," the invisible benefactor who has become every soldier's best friend. On September 15, 1961, the 87th Congress of the United States adopts the following Resolution: "Resolved by the Senate with the House of Representatives concurring, the Congress salutes 'Uncle Sam' Wilson of Troy, New York, as the progenitor of America's national symbol of 'Uncle Sam.'"

Johnny Appleseed and Uncle Sam. Just a couple of kids who met one summer on a farm outside Mason, New Hampshire. Just a couple of kids like you and me. ✒

MORNING GLORY
HEAVENLY BLUE

Seed Store
Wilmington,   N. C.

89

A Pinpoint in the Darkness

There is no sky so big as the one that covers the ocean. For twelve days, there has been nothing to see.

I wait patiently until day's end to ask my question, because I know the captain is a busy man. Now staring at his silhouette against the star-studded skies of midnight, I anxiously await his answer.

Framed in darkness, the shadowy captain points an inky finger upward and starboard and says to me, "Polaris does not move."

"But Captain Columbus," I respond quickly, "I don't understand."

Never lowering his finger, the captain continues: "Fools watch the waves and make decisions according to ever-changing circumstances, but a wise captain charts his course by a star which does not move.* When your journey is long and the way before you is rough, never take your eyes off the North Star, boy. Focus your vision on beautiful, unwavering, constant Polaris."

Are you making decisions by the actions of the waves, or have you charted your course according to the principles and ideals you believe in?

See ch. 61, "Change Is Inevitable, Growth Is Optional."

Story attributed to Tom Monte myth 9-year stowaway aboard Santa

* The Native Americans who awaited Columbus knew Polaris as "The Star That Does Not Walk Around."

Ideals are like the stars. We will never reach them, but like the mariners on the sea, we chart our course by them.

Carl Schurz, 1869
(Close friend of Abraham Lincoln)

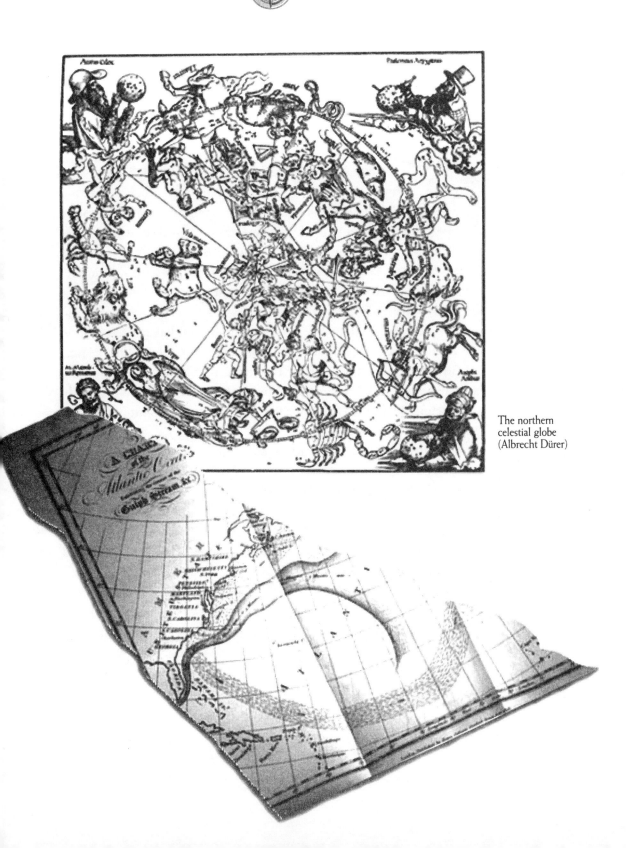

The northern
celestial globe
(Albrecht Dürer)

90

Teedie the Asthmatic

eedie is a scrawny teenage boy with buck teeth and asthma, but he has the heart of an overcomer. While the other boys sneak glances at Connie Boden, Teedie boldly walks over and asks if he might come by to visit sometime. "Certainly!" says the stunningly attractive Miss Boden, "How about a picnic tomorrow?" Now it's the other boys who are gasping for air.

At 5 AM the following morning, Teedie plops into his rowboat and throws his slight weight into the oars. It's several miles across the bay to where the Bodens live, but Connie Boden has invited Teedie to a picnic, and he has no intention of being late. Three hours later, Teedie steps out of his rowboat to realize that he is fully two hours early. Exhausted from his rowing, Teedie lies on a rock and promptly falls asleep. He awakens an hour later to find that his boat has drifted two hundred yards from shore.

Resourceful and self-reliant, Teedie places his clothes neatly in a pile, swims naked to his boat and rows it back to shore, thinking, "Never ask for help when you don't have to have it." Now dripping wet and bone weary, Teedie stacks his clothes in the boat and lies down naked on the rock to dry.

The sound of distant voices awakens him. Connie Boden and another girl are coming through the trees — and Teedie's boat has again drifted away! Teedie dives beneath the dock to hide. Later, a naked and weary Teedie swims out to his boat to begin his long, silent journey home. "I never got to the picnic," he thinks, " but I didn't have to ask for help, either. Everything considered, not a bad day."

Why didn't Teedie ask for help, you ask? If Teedie had simply asked someone to row him to his boat instead of swimming to it naked, his story would have ended with a picnic instead of rowing home alone, right?

Yes, this is altogether true. But if Teedie had been the kind of boy who was quick to ask for help, he wouldn't have been the man to lead the Rough Riders up impossible San Juan Hill. He wouldn't have been the lovable renegade who became our twenty-sixth president, and we certainly would never have carved his face into a granite mountain in South Dakota.

Teedie will live forever on Rushmore with Washington, Jefferson, and Lincoln because America saw in him the embodiment of her own soul: bold enough to attempt the unlikely, resourceful to the point of nakedness, reckless to the point of near drowning, but with the heart of an overcomer. Everything considered, not a bad way to live.

What impossible thing will you attempt today?

A determined soul will do more with a rusty monkey wrench than a loafer will accomplish with all the tools in a machine shop.

Rupert Hughes

91

Choose to Be Lucky!

I decided to become a coin collector the summer after my second grade, and my decision became official when I put it in a letter to my grandmother. When my father came home that night, I asked if I could search through his pocket change for interesting coins, "because I'm a coin collector."

Dad had only one coin that was even a little bit unusual. It was a 1955 penny, only ten years old, but it had two additional fives plainly stamped into the date. I took the penny and searched for a special place to put it. For some reason I'll never understand, I decided to pull up the air conditioner vent from the floor of my bedroom at 404 Grandview Boulevard, where I tucked the penny under the revealed edge of the carpet. I then replaced the air conditioner vent into its hole and completely forgot about coin collecting until two weeks later, when I received a book about coin values as a gift from my grandmother. On page one was a huge photo of my penny.

The publishers of the coin guide were offering a hundred dollars for pennies like mine. They called it a 1955 double die. Coin books today say my penny will bring from five hundred to two thousand dollars and that it's the third-rarest penny in U.S. history. But I forgot where I put it. I didn't remember pulling up the air conditioner vent and tucking the penny under the carpet.

Until seventeen years later. I knocked on the door at 404 Grandview Boulevard only to learn that the carpet had been changed four years earlier. No penny.

Am I the luckiest person in the world for finding that penny on my very first day of coin collecting, or am I the unluckiest person in the world for losing it?

I choose to believe I'm lucky. I consider myself so lucky, in fact, that I never buy lottery tickets because I don't feel it would be fair to all the people who don't have my amazing luck. Do you have this kind of luck? You can if you'd like.

An ancient scholar wrote, "As a man thinks in his heart, so is he," and I completely agree. We are the sum total of our thoughts. If you are what you think, why not think yourself lucky? It's easy to do! Just take a moment to look around and notice all the good things in your life and be glad for them.

You are lucky. Very lucky. Good things happen to you for no reason at all! You are amazingly, unbelievably, mind-bendingly lucky.

Don't ever forget it. 🎋

92

UFO Taxi

I've got to see one more autumn," he said. "I need to sit under a tree in a sweater and eat a crisp, fresh apple." I'm in Palm Beach, Florida, riding in the back seat of a taxicab driven by a man named Brennan, who I'm pretty sure is a leprechaun. (Remember the character on the Saturday morning TV ad who says, "They're after me Lucky Charms! They're magically delicious!"? I think maybe this is that guy.)

I've never enjoyed a cab ride more.

It's a long way to where I'm going, and I'm glad, because Brennan tells the kind of stories that only the Irish can tell, each one ending with a reminiscent sigh and him saying wistfully, "That was a good day."

After one such story, I startle Brennan out of his reverie by asking, "What are you going to do in Oregon after you've eaten the apple?" Brennan pauses, then decides to answer. "Twenty-eight years ago," he says, "I bought a Les Paul goldtop guitar and, other than the clothes on my back, that guitar is my only possession." A moment passes in silence before he continues, "I've been writing songs since the day I bought that guitar, but I've never finished a single one of 'em. I plan to sit under the tree, eat the apple, and finish a song. . . . That will be my best day."

Percy Ross is an eighty-two-year-old multimillionaire philanthropist who writes a syndicated column called "Thanks a Million," through which he dispenses weekly gifts and fatherly advice. During one of my visits with Percy, I mentioned that I've noticed his gifts tend to be rather modest, considering that he's a multimillionaire: new pool sticks for some guys in a nursing home; a wig for a woman undergoing chemotherapy; a pair of cowboy boots for a city kid who dreams of horses. "Heck, Percy, I could afford to give away most of the things you give to people." He answers with a twinkle in his eye, "I'm glad you're finally catching on. That's exactly what I hope to inspire people to do. It's amazing what a small gift to a stranger can do to change his life — and yours."

On September 4 at precisely 11:50 AM, Delta Airlines flight 1625 will deboard its passengers in Portland, Oregon. Among them will be a leprechaun.

I'm anxious to hear his song.

In this chapter, the mental image of a leprechaun surprises Broca (see ch. 30) and makes the story more memorable. The leprechaun is used as both FMI and LMI (see p. 117).

The greatest things ever done on earth have been done little by little.

Thomas Guthrie

93

History's Greatest Hoax

ill is a merchant, married to the woman who became pregnant when they were both eighteen. He lives an obscure life and dies at age fifty-two, having never learned to read or write.

Edward is a writer who calls himself "the Seventeenth Earl of Oxford." He is an educated man with a passion for tennis and is well versed in the intrigues of politics. Ed writes deep and biting satire. His wit has a razor's edge.

Orphaned at twelve, Edward is reared by a high-ranking government official. At the age of twenty-one, Ed defies convention by marrying the official's daughter. The hero of Edward's next story also marries his guardian's daughter.

Three years later, Edward is on a ship when it is attacked and its passengers held for ransom. Likewise, the hero in Ed's next story is captured by pirates and held for ransom.

Eight months after Edward leaves on a yearlong journey, his wife has a baby daughter. Upon his return, he falsely accuses his wife of infidelity and refuses to live with her. Five years later, Edward comes to his senses and his loving wife forgives him his ridiculous accusations. Several of Ed's later stories feature a woman wrongfully accused of adultery, but in each story the woman forgives her husband.

During the five years Edward is separated from his wife, he has an affair with another woman and is physically attacked by one of her friends, resulting in a blood feud between the two families. This feud becomes the foundation for the biggest story Ed will ever write.

Learning of his intentions to publish, government officials ask to read Ed's stories before they go into print. This is important only because Edward really is the Seventeenth Earl of Oxford and dozens of the characters in his stories are modeled after people still in government. Horrified by what might happen if the stories were published in Ed's own name, they offer him an amazing stipend for life if he will agree never to claim authorship of the work. Ed immediately agrees and chooses a name at random, never once suspecting it to be the name of an obscure merchant on the other side of town.

Would Edward de Vere have accepted his government's liberal pension and inserted a name other than his own had he known that future generations would believe an illiterate merchant to be the greatest author who ever lived? For Edward did not sign his work as "Bill," but chose to use the more formal name of William. William Shakespeare.

That every word doth almost tell my name,
Showing their birth, and where they did proceed.

William Shakespeare, Sonnet 76

94
Oscar

write these words in the early morning hours of April 18, 1998, having just encountered fresh proof of my Theory of Universal Knowledge, which, you may recall, states, "There is a time for every idea, and when that time has come, the idea will spring into the minds of several people simultaneously."

While perusing books of pithy quotes, I noticed that many of the best were followed by the name "Oscar Wilde." Intrigued, I learned that Oscar Wilde was a flamboyant young Irishman who became a superstar of writing, fashion, and wit during the late 1800s. Oscar understood the power of words and used them with the skill of a master.

The English-speaking world of 1883 lay prostrate at young Oscar's feet. Everyone wanted to be in Oscar's inner circle. He married for love, had two adorable sons, and was later charmed by a young house guest. Nine years after, this man who had lived with the world at his feet died without a dollar or a friend. His story was one of the most amazing I had ever encountered. I thought, "I'm going to write a screenplay about the meteoric rise and fall of this talented and troubled young man. I can't believe his incredible story hasn't been made into a movie."

As I gathered the details of Oscar's life, I became more and more intrigued and excited. Then I stumbled across an Internet website announcing that *Wilde*, a new motion picture from Samuelson Entertainment, would be released in the U.S. in two weeks. Universal Knowledge strikes again.

See "Theory of Universal Knowledge," p. 193.

From what I gleaned from the website, I fear *Wilde* will be little more than a one-dimensional portrayal of Oscar as a homosexual martyr. If I am right, the movie will never become more than a favorite among America's gay community. Properly told, Oscar's story has the potential to be much, much more. The true story of Oscar Wilde is far more riveting than the story of the *Titanic*.

As I sit at my desk this fine spring morning, my plan is to wait until *Wilde* has come and gone. I will then tell Oscar's story as I believe it truly happened. In the meantime, I will leave you to consider two of his most revealing quotes.

Near the end, Oscar wrote of himself:

I was a man who stood in symbolic relations to the art and culture of my age. . . . The gods had given me almost everything.

I had genius, a distinguished name, high social position, brilliancy, intellectual daring; I made art a philosophy, and philosophy an art; I altered the minds of men and the colour of things; there was nothing I said or did that did not make people wonder. . . .

I treated art as the supreme reality, and life as a mere mode of fiction; I awoke the imagination of my century so that it created myth and legend around me. I summed up all systems in a phrase, and all existence in an epigram.

And to the young house guest who had charmed him and triggered his tragic downfall:

Ah, Robbie, when we are dead and buried in our porphyry tombs, and the trumpet of the Last Judgment is sounded, I shall turn and whisper to you, "Robbie, Robbie, let us pretend we do not hear it."

95

What Price Success?

His neck caught under a spring-loaded bail, the little mouse looks up at me with anxious eyes. He is extremely uncomfortable, but breathing. Is it my imagination, or do I hear a tiny, choked voice saying, "You can keep the cheese, sir, just please let me out of the trap"?

My suspicion is that this little mouse has been to a seminar where a razzle-dazzle motivator encouraged him to tape a picture of his goal over his bathroom mirror. Staring at the photo of the cheese each day, the mouse chants the motivator's mantra, "You can do it, you're a winner, you can do it, you're a winner," and of course he is right. The little mouse soon gets what he wants, never pausing to consider the wire bail that might come with it. (His new goal is simply to take that picture off the bathroom mirror.)

The little mouse was focused on the cheese and committed to achieving it, and although focus and commitment are essential to success, overfocus and overcommitment are commonly called obsession and addiction — neither of which leads to happiness.

Like all of us, you are spending the minutes, hours, and days of your life in the pursuit of something that you are buying with your very life. Have you inspected the package? Are you chasing what you really want, or might there be a spring-loaded bail attached to the cheese?

See ch. 14, "The Changing Face of the Rich."

Too many people today are focused on what they think they want without giving a thought to what they don't want that might come with it. Ignore the sales trainers who urge you to tape your favorite magazine ads onto your bathroom mirror. I can promise you that nothing clipped from a magazine is worthy of your life.

What do you really want?

There is too much stress today
on material things. I try to teach
my children not so much the value
of cents, but a sense of value.

Morris Franklin

If I had only known, I would have
been a locksmith.

Albert Einstein

96

Harold and Jeff

arold moved in across the street from us when Pennie and I were twenty-two years old. He was a gentle soul, about ten years older than me, and he wore his hair in a style that was strangely out of date. I considered Harold to be the last of the Woodstock hippies — a breed largely extinct by 1980. Sometimes in the evening I would walk across the street to help Harold work on his car.

One Sunday afternoon, a stranger knocked on my door to tell me that Harold was in jail and wanted to know if I could come downtown with a hundred and fifty dollars in cash to post his bail. It seems Harold had run a red light and wasn't carrying a driver's license. By miraculous coincidence, I actually had a hundred and fifty dollars, so I headed to the police station with it.

As I drove Harold home, he told me that his real name was Jeff and that he was an escaped convict. He said he was lucky that government agencies aren't open on Sundays, or a computer match of his fingerprints would have already revealed his true identity. He said that each time he had been recaptured during the past twelve years, it was because he had been pulled over without a driver's license. He said, "Last time it took them less than two hours before an officer came to my cell and called me by name. My real name."

The silence grew uncomfortable. Then I finally got up the nerve to ask, "Why were you originally sent to jail?" Jeff smiled a bitter-sweet smile. "I ran away from a bad situation at home in 1968, when I was eighteen years old. After walking down the highway for several hours with my thumb in the air, I spotted a large barn near a farm-house. I came out of that barn carrying a five-gallon can of gas, which I planned to offer to whoever who would give me a ride. About ten minutes later, the county sheriff arrested me. It turns out the farmer had seen me do it and he really hated guys with long hair. Especially ones that had just stolen his favorite five-gallon can."

After another uncomfortable silence, Jeff continued: "I escaped from county jail in a cart full of dirty laundry. When I was recaptured, my sentence was lengthened because of the escape and they sent me off to prison. One day I went over the wall. Every time I've been recaptured since then, I've always gone over the wall."

With eyes like silver dollars and my mouth hanging open like a dolt, I whispered, "How do you get over the wall?"

"It's easy," said Jeff. "Getting over the wall isn't really that hard when you've lost your fear of death. It's never really the wall that holds you. It's the fear of dying."

It was just then that we pulled into my driveway. Jeff got out of the car without a word, walked across the street to his house and emerged moments later carrying a duffel bag. He then repaid me the hundred and fifty dollars and asked if I would drive him to the bus station. When we arrived, he said, "When the police come looking for me on Monday morning, go ahead and tell them that you took me to the bus station. I don't want you to have to lie." We said goodbye, and I never saw Jeff again.

I learned from Jeff that running away from trouble is never really a good idea. I think that Harold would agree.

Real difficulties can be overcome; it is only the imaginary ones that are unconquerable.

Theodore N. Vail

97

Golden Apples

Holding my charts in a manila folder, the doctor said, "I don't know how to tell you this, but we've discovered that you have a hereditary condition for which there is no treatment." When I asked the doctor if my condition had a name, he nodded and said, "Yes, it's called stupidity." Then he turned on his heel and walked out of the emergency room.

I've never been completely sure why the doctor said what he did, but it might be because I fell off a motorcycle after falling asleep at sixty miles an hour. As I lay motionless in the middle of a winding road halfway between my office and my home, an unfortunate lady came sweeping around the corner and ran over me before she could react. Luckily, I was already unconscious at the time. I woke up in the emergency room an hour and fifteen minutes later. "Pennie," I said, "Did I buy the $2,500 deductible policy, or the $5,000 deductible?"

You want to hear the strangest part of all? It wasn't the doctor, the pain, the money, or the hospital food which convinced me to give up motorcycles. It was a carefully worded note from a friend: "Dear Roy, I think you should give up motorcycles and start collecting ink pens. Please find enclosed the most interesting pen I've ever seen. Sincerely, Skip Robbins."

Skip wasn't trying to be cute or witty. The genuine nature of his concern was evidenced by the fact that he had enclosed a very expensive, truly remarkable ink pen. The kind of pen that would inspire a collection. Skip felt strongly that I should give up motorcycles, but he also knew that I would resist any attempt to be shamed, begged, reasoned with, or browbeaten.

From the time I was a young boy, I have puzzled over the meaning of a phrase from an often-quoted passage in the book of Proverbs.

A modern paraphrase of the passage would read, "To speak just the right word at just the right time in just the right way is like apples of gold in pitchers of silver." I doubt if Skip Robbins can explain why the writer of Proverbs chose to use the odd image of golden apples in a silver pitcher, but Skip obviously knows how to do what the writer was trying to say.

The next time you fear a person is about to make a serious mistake, speak up. You don't have to argue, criticize, or say more than a word or two. A single word of genuine concern from a friend is a very powerful thing. 🐾

See ch. 1, "The Energy of Words."

98

What I Learned at a Bar Mitzvah

Aaron Grosbard read from the Torah, and then we all threw candy at him. Even before the candy landed, the aisles were filled with little kids scrambling to rearm themselves. Candy and laughter filled the air in a flying candy skirmish, then all the kids sat down and the Temple service continued.

Noting the bewildered look on my face, the lady sitting next to me leaned over and said, "The Mitzvah happened the moment Aaron read from the Torah. Aaron is now recognized as an adult."

I always thought a Bar Mitzvah would be like a birthday party, an event unto itself with layers and layers of ritual and the spotlight always on Aaron. What I learned in New York City is that the Jewish passage into manhood occurs when a young man is allowed to participate as one of the adults who reads aloud from the Torah on a Sabbath. The honor is simply that he is allowed to be part of the whole.

That night, in evening gown and tuxedo at Aaron's reception, Pennie and I watched hundreds of little kids, old people, parents, and teenagers dance their celebration of Aaron's arrival into manhood. Experiencing their interaction as a community, our admiration for Jewish people rose to a whole new level.

So what did I learn in New York City? I learned that simply being included is a very important thing. A thing worth being celebrated. A thing that you and I should never again take for granted. I learned in New York City how important it is to belong.

Where do you belong? If you were to write a detailed description of your life without ever making reference to your occupation, what would your description say? (Remember: Who you are is never defined by what you do.) Your identity as a person is defined only by your loyalties and then expressed through your relationships.

Why not make an exercise of it? Why not invest a few minutes to investigate who you are? Write on a sheet of paper: I am the friend of . . . (How many names can you put here?) I am the extremely close friend of . . . (How many people?) I am the soul mate of . . . (Who?) I appreciate and enjoy . . . (A good book? Old cars? Broadway musicals?) How many things can you write?

In doing this exercise, you may learn that you need to give more of yourself to others, because too much of your identity has been wrapped up in your occupation.

You may also learn that you are in the middle of a pretty wonderful life. 🙏

The Wizard's Secret Formula for Traveling to New York City

1. Fly into Newark, New Jersey.

2. Drive 17 minutes down the New Jersey Turnpike toward Manhattan, then

3. take the very last NJ exit before going through the Lincoln Tunnel.

4. Follow the exit ramp to the dead end at the bottom of the hill.

5. Turn right.

6. Drive about half a mile, then

7. turn left and drive the remaining quarter-mile to the river.

8. Look for the Sheraton Suites at Lincoln Harbor in Weehawken. This is where you will stay.

The ferry stops at the Sheraton every quarter-hour and will motor you across the Hudson to Manhattan in just seven delightful minutes. From there, a cab will take you wherever you need to go. From the hotel each night, you'll view a city of illuminated crystal framed by the inky black Hudson beneath and the pitch-black sky above. It's truly an amazing sight. If New Yorkers ever once saw their city from the Jersey shore, they'd all immediately move to New Jersey.

99

Huebner's Fourth Rule of Mountaineering: Never Turn Your Back on Your Partner

Most of us eventually learn a key bit of wisdom: the highest road to inner peace and lasting success lies through personal loyalty. To accept responsibility for the welfare of another, and then to guard that person's interest as though it were your own, is the mark of a happy and vibrant life. By manifesting loyalty to another, you learn as well to recognize and trust in that person's loyalty.

Are you a dependable employee? A loyal partner? A faithful friend? Happiest is the one who can answer with confidence, "Yes. Yes. And Yes."

Huebner's Six Rules
of Mountaineering:
See pp. 37–38.

There is one element that is worth its weight in gold and that is loyalty. It will cover a multitude of weaknesses.

Philip D. Armour

100
New Kid

y mother and I pack our few possessions into boxes we have found behind the grocery store, then drive to the house we've rented in the poorest part of town. I stack the boxes on the kitchen floor, then go in search of the sweet fragrance that hangs like mist in the still summer air. Stepping into the backyard, I see that honeysuckle vines wrap a chicken-wire fence in a thick carpet of green leaves and yellow flowers. I stare at the honeysuckle and smile into the sunlight.

Across the fence an old woman is working in her vegetable garden, watching me in the way that old people sometimes do. After a few moments, she straightens her back and says, "Climb over. I've got something to show you." I hop the fence where the honeysuckle is thinnest and follow her into a tiny garage where she points to a cardboard box. "My son loved those books, but he's gone to college now. He said to give them to an eleven-year-old boy. Are you eleven?" I nod that I surely am.

The box contains all the adventures of Tom Corbett, Space Cadet, and inside each cover is a name written in blue ink: "Sammy Haggard." It's a signature that will forever be etched in my memory because Sammy Haggard made it possible for me to spend an entire summer traveling the solar system in a spaceship called Polaris, with a new friend named Tom Corbett.

When you're the new kid and you don't know anyone and your parents are getting a divorce, Jupiter is a pretty great place to be.

Thank you, Sammy Haggard. I'll always remember your name. 🦎

100 + 1

A Letter from William Lederer to Admiral David McDonald

hile traveling in France, William Lederer witnessed an incident involving an American sailor that touched him so deeply he sent the following letter to the chief of naval operations in Washington, D.C. The letter is taken from the amazing book, *Letters of a Nation,* edited by our pal, Andrew Carroll.

Admiral David L. McDonald, USN
Chief of Naval Operations
Washington, D.C.

Dear Admiral McDonald,

Eighteen people asked me to write this letter to you. Last year at Christmas time, my wife, three boys and I were in France, on our way from Paris to Nice. For five wretched days everything had gone wrong. Our hotels were "tourist traps," our rented car broke down; we were all restless and irritable in the crowded car. On Christmas Eve, when we checked into our hotel in Nice, there was no Christmas spirit in our hearts.

It was raining and cold when we went out to eat. We found a drab little restaurant shoddily decorated for the holiday. Only five tables were occupied. There were two German couples, two French families, and an American sailor, by himself. In the corner a piano player listlessly played Christmas music.

I was too tired and miserable to leave. I noticed that the other customers were eating in stony silence. The only person who seemed

Remem
the Am
who we
impress
by the s
in LasVa
that sa
"You mu
present
win"?
Same

happy was the American sailor. While eating, he was writing a letter, and a half-smile lighted his face.

My wife ordered our meal in French. The waiter brought us the wrong thing. I scolded my wife for being stupid. The boys defended her, and I felt even worse.

Then, at the table with the French family on our left, the father slapped one of his children for some minor infraction, and the boy began to cry.

On our right, the German wife began berating her husband.

All of us were interrupted by an unpleasant blast of cold air. Through the front door came an old flower woman. She wore a dripping, tattered overcoat, and shuffled in on wet, rundown shoes. She went from one table to the other.

"Flowers, monsieur? Only one franc."

No one bought any.

Wearily she sat down at a table between the sailor and us. To the waiter she said, "A bowl of soup. I haven't sold a flower all afternoon." To the piano player she said hoarsely, "Can you imagine, Joseph, soup on Christmas Eve?"

He pointed to his empty "tipping plate."

The young sailor finished his meal and got up to leave. Putting on his coat, he walked over to the flower woman's table.

"Happy Christmas," he said, smiling and picking out two corsages. "How much are they?"

"Two francs, monsieur."

Pressing one of the small corsages flat, he put it into the letter he had written, then handed the woman a twenty-franc note.

"I don't have change, monsieur." She said. "I'll get some from the waiter."

"No, ma'am." Said the sailor, leaning over and kissing the ancient cheek. "This is my Christmas present to you."

Then he came to our table, holding the other corsage in front of him. "Sir," he said to me, "may I have permission to present these flowers to your beautiful daughter?"

In one quick motion he gave my wife the corsage, wished us a Merry Christmas and departed.

Everyone had stopped eating. Everyone had been watching the sailor. Everyone was silent.

A few seconds later Christmas exploded throughout the restaurant like a bomb.

The old flower woman jumped up, waving the twenty-franc note, shouted to the piano player, "Joseph, my Christmas present! And you shall have half so you can have a feast too."

The piano player began to belt out "Good King Wenceslaus," beating the keys with magic hands.

My wife waved her corsage in time to the music. She appeared twenty years younger. She began to sing, and our three sons joined her, bellowing with enthusiasm.

"Gut! Gut!" shouted the Germans. They began singing in German.

The waiter embraced the flower woman. Waving their arms, they sang in French.

The Frenchman who had slapped the boy beat rhythm with his fork against a bottle. The lad climbed on his lap, singing in a youthful soprano.

A few hours earlier eighteen persons had been spending a miserable evening. It ended up being the happiest, the very best Christmas Eve, they had ever experienced.

This, Admiral McDonald, is what I am writing you about. As the top man in the Navy, you should know about the very special gift that the U.S. Navy gave to my family, to me and to the other people in that French restaurant. Because your young sailor had Christmas spirit in his soul, he released the love and joy that had been smothered within us by anger and disappointment. He gave us Christmas.

Thank you, Sir, very much.

Merry Christmas,

Bill Lederer

Part the Final

Glossary, Index, and Other Vital Information

In Which the Wizard Provides
Tools with Which the Student Can
Synthesize Knowledge and Wisdom

The Wizard's Glossary

Every industry has its jargon, and advertising has some of the wackiest. Here are a few of the terms you may hear, with a loose interpretation of what they mean.

account executive: sales rep.

agate line: in newspaper, a depth of 1/14 column inch. A standard newspaper page will contain approximately 2,400 agate lines (300 lines per column times eight columns).

Arbitron: a research company that measures the comparative audience of radio stations.

avail: "available unsold inventory," in full. Broadcast and cable reps typically refer to their unsold ads as "avails."

average quarter-hour: in broadcast, the number of people likely to be reached during the average commercial break.

bleed: in print and outdoor advertising, the process of printing all the way to the edge of the page, leaving no white border or "blanking area." See "poster."

branding: see chapter 7, "What Is Branding?"

BTA: a broadcast ad scheduling term meaning "best time available," technically better than ROS (run of schedule) since it promises to deliver the best of all the station's unsold inventory, though most people mistakenly use the terms interchangeably.

bulletin: a billboard fourteen feet high and forty-eight feet wide, once called a "painted bulletin" or "painted display."

certificate of mailing: a slip provided by the post office certifying that a certain number of pieces of mail were actually sent. Often presented by direct-mail companies as proof they actually sent your mailing.

column inch: a measure of space in print advertising that is one column wide by one inch deep.

commissionable rate: an ad rate that provides for a commission to be paid to the advertising agency that places the order. Usually the agency collects the "gross" rate from its client, then pays the "net" rate (usually the gross rate minus 15 percent) to the medium.

copy: the words in an ad.

cost per point: the cost of reaching one percent of the population one time. Often abbreviated as CPP.

cost per thousand: the cost of reaching one thousand people one time each. Occasionally abbreviated as CPM (M for the Latin "milli," meaning "thousand").

cume: from "cumulative"; the total number of individuals who tune into a particular station within a specified period of time.

daypart: in broadcast, a time window. The five radio dayparts are morning drive, midday, afternoon drive, evening, and overnight.

direct account: an advertiser with whom a medium interacts directly, meaning that no advertising agency is involved.

extension: In outdoor advertising, a protrusion that extends outside the standard rectangle, creating a dramatic effect. Extensions are available only on bulletins, never on posters.

frequency: the number of times your ad will reach the same person in a given period.

grips: slang term for gross rating points or "GRPs."

gross impression: the effect of having reached one person one time, through any medium. Total gross impressions are calculated by multiplying your reach by your frequency.

gross rates: ad rates that are "commissionable" to recognized ad agencies, usually meaning that the rates will be discounted by a 15 percent commission paid to the agency for having assisted in making the sale to the advertiser.

gross rating points: the total gross impressions made by an ad campaign, expressed as a percentage of the population. In theory, a campaign that achieves 100 GRPs has reached the equivalent of 100 percent of the population of an area, one time. In reality, 100 GRPs can just as easily mean that you reached 10 percent of the population 10 times each, or 1 percent 100 times. (The Wizard never calculates gross rating points because they tell him nothing that he can use.)

horizontal scheduling: the practice of scheduling a broadcast ad to air at essentially the same time each day in an attempt to reach the same persons over and over.

house account: an advertiser on whose account no commission is paid to a sales rep; usually, an account that has been given discounted rates because it requires very little maintenance.

linage: another term for column inches, but expressed in agate lines.

mechanical requirements: the submission requirements of a newspaper, magazine, or outdoor advertising company.

MobilTrak: a "black box" device that records the radio station to which a car radio is tuned as it drives past a specific point.

net rate: an advertising rate that is neither discountable nor commissionable.

Nielsen: a research company that measures the comparative viewership of television shows.

open rate: in print advertising, the rate paid by an advertiser who has made no commitment to a bulk purchase of linage or column inches.

optimum effective scheduling (OES): in the Wizard's opinion, a complex calculation that is performed to answer a largely irrelevant question. See ch. 58, "Radio Scheduling."

plant: the physical structure supporting a billboard.

POP: "point of purchase," a term denoting a physical attempt, usually in the form of signage or other type of display, made to influence the shopper while in the store.

poster: a temporary billboard (usually thirty to sixty days) that is printed on strips of paper, then applied to a mounting surface. See "thirty-sheet poster."

preemptible: an arrangement whereby an ad is scheduled on the condition that it can be "bumped" in the event another advertiser is willing to pay a higher rate for the same avail. See "avail."

public relations (PR) firm: while an advertising agency deals with a medium's sales department, a public relations firm deals with its news department. "Advertising" is media exposure that you purchase; the job of a PR firm is to get you media exposure for free. (PR people and advertising people are *not* interchangeable. I've never met anyone who could do both jobs well.)

rate card: physically, a sheet that lists advertising rates, but often used as a slang term meaning "asking price."

reach: the total number of different people reached by an ad campaign.

rep: media salesperson. See "account executive."

ROP: "run of paper." In newspaper, an arrangement whereby the newspaper has the freedom to place your ad wherever it wants.

ROS: in broadcasting, "run of schedule," a term that means your ad will run somewhere in a twenty-four-hour day — or maybe tomorrow.

rotary bulletin: in outdoor advertising, an arrangement whereby your billboard is moved periodically to a new location, which is usually a good idea, since a bulletin that stays in one location too long becomes effectively invisible. There are no rotary posters, because posters are printed on paper and cannot be moved from site to site. See "poster."

rotator package: in television, a term that means the station wants to sell you some of its less desirable avails by "rotating" your ads all over the schedule.

short rate: a penalty paid by an advertiser upon his breach of a bulk advertising agreement. Usually calculated by determining the difference between the contract rate and the earned rate, multiplied by the amount of advertising that was actually used.

showing: a term in outdoor advertising that roughly communicates impact. A "100 showing" may be one billboard in a tiny town or several hundred billboards in Los Angeles. In effect, a "100 showing" is a package designed to be seen by virtually everyone in an area, several times in a month. There are also "50 showings," "25 showings," and so forth.

slick, or ad slick: in newspaper, a camera-ready ad. The term comes from the shiny surface of the special paper on which such ads were originally printed.

snipe: the strip across the bottom of a thirty-sheet poster containing the name of a local retailer. Most often used when the poster has been provided by a manufacturer whose product the retailer carries.

standby: a designation referring to ads that are ready to insert at a moment's notice if last-minute ad space should suddenly become available. Though not all newspapers offer standby rates, many will insert your quarter-page or larger ad for half the regular price, provided you have a camera-ready ad on file in their office. Outdoor companies will also occasionally agree to sell standby posters, provided you give them a stock of thirty-sheet posters that they can apply in random locations as unsold plants become available.

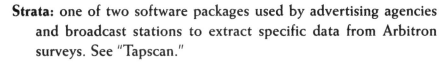

Strata: one of two software packages used by advertising agencies and broadcast stations to extract specific data from Arbitron surveys. See "Tapscan."

tabloid, or tab: a nonstandard newspaper size that has five columns per page, fourteen inches deep, compared to a standard page of eight columns, twenty-one to twenty-two inches deep.

TAP: "total audience plan," radio's version of the rotator. Beyond this, the definition gets fuzzy. While one station may have a "three-part TAP" consisting of one spot in morning drive, a second during midday, and a third during afternoon drive, the next station may schedule its "three-part TAP" as one spot between 6 AM and 7 PM, a second spot between 7 PM and midnight, and a third between midnight and 6 AM. There are also "four-part TAPs" and "five-part TAPs." Always ask your rep to define precisely what type of rotation his station considers "TAP."

Tapscan: the other "reach and frequency" calculation software used by advertising agencies and broadcast stations to extract specific data from Arbitron surveys. See "Strata."

thirty-sheet poster: a billboard (see "poster") twelve feet high and twenty-five feet wide.

TOMA: a research firm measuring category dominance or "top of mind awareness" in each of several dozen business categories in cities nationwide.

traffic: the department in charge of scheduling ads.

unit pricing: in radio, the practice of selling sixty-second ads and thirty-second ads for the same price.

vertical scheduling: the practice of scheduling a series of broadcast ads to air in a single day in an attempt to reach the same person repeatedly, the principal goal being to increase the ratio of ad repetition to listener sleep.

The Wizard's Index

Brain. *See also* Memory
  auditory association area of, 50, 51, 55
  auditory cortex of, 50, 51
  auditory pattern activation and encoding, 48–49
  Broca's area of, 51, 52–53, 70–71, 73, 83, 110–1
  diagram of, 51
  mental images and, 70–71, 73, 116–9
  motor association cortex of, 52
  prefrontal cortex of, 51, 52
  ratio of sensory receptors to brain synapses, 44, 64–65
  visual association area of, 50, 51
  visual cortex of, 50, 51
  Wernicke's area of, 50, 51, 52, 70
Branding, 22–23, 76, 98, 192
Bravery, 36–39, 86–87, 104, 188–9
Breakthrough, 156–9
Brennan, 202, 203
Brentwood Bank, 144
Broad rotator, 130
Broca, Paul, 52
Broca's area, 51, 52–53, 70–71, 73, 83, 110–1
BTA (best time available), 224
Budget for advertising, 120–1, 124
Bulletin, 224
Business management. *See also* Sales
  banking and banker terminology, 144–8, 158–9
  breakthrough and, 156–9
  CEO's vision, 143
  complaints from customers, 176–7
  employees and, 141–12, 149, 160, 167–71, 174–5
  exceptional service from employees, 174–5
  firing employees, 170–1
  inventory turn and, 150–1
  lighting and, 140–1
  merchandising, 141
  mountaineering rules applied to, 138, 160, 163, 178
  and regression to the mean, 172–3
  sales success, 154–5
  salespeople and, 141–2, 149
  and World Inside Your Door, 140–2, 149
  and World of the Executive Office, 143
  and World Outside Your Door, 139
  writing classified ads for employment, 167–9
Businessquakes, 143

Cable television, 131
Cameron, James, 57
Capitalism, 148
Carlyle, Thomas, 95
Carroll, Andrew (Andy), 110, 218
Carter, Sharon, 103
Cary, Clay, 144–5, 147, 158
Cash flow, 148

Category dominance, 24
Category killers, 84–85
CD player, 172
Certificate of mailing, 224–5
Change as inevitable, 134–5
Chapman, Johnny, 194–5
Chevrolet, 124
Children's books, 152, 153, 192, 193, 217
Christmas, 218–20
Chrysler, 34
Cicero, 193
Circuit City, 24, 84
Clancy, Kevin, 32
Classified ads for employment, 167–9
Clayton, Lawrence, 103
Clerks versus sales professionals, 153
Clichés, 15
Clients. *See also* Customers
  as always right/wrong, 17
  overtargeting to, 18, 25, 123
  putting clients in ads, 34–35
Close rate, 148, 149
Clothing, 34, 68, 164–6
Cohen, Ben, 78
Coin collecting, 200
Coke, 124
Columbus, Christopher, 196
Column inch, 225
Commissionable rate, 225
Comparison shopping, 84
Complaints from customers, 176–7
Consistency for associative memory, 22–23
Coping with Depression (Carter and Clayton), 103
Copy, 225
Corbett, Tom, 217
Corcoran, Jeff, 84
Cost per point (CPP), 225
Courage, 36–39, 86–87, 104, 188–9
CPP (cost per point), 225
Creative writing, 114, 115
Criminal activities, 162–3
Critical equation for scheduling, 129
Crusoe, Robinson, 44
Cullen, John, 122
Cume, 225
Current ratio, 145
Customers
  as always right/wrong, 17
  complaints by, 176–7
  as complete human beings, 30–31
  extraordinary service for, 174–5
  identification of, 25
  overtargeting to, 18, 25, 123

Grosbard, Aaron, 214
Gross impression, 225
Gross margin, 148
Gross profit, 148
Gross rates, 226
Gross rating points (GRPs), 16, 106, 122–3, 225, 226
GRPs (gross rating points), 16, 106, 122–3, 225, 226
Guthrie, Thomas, 203

Häagen-Dazs, 78
Haggard, Sammy, 217
Half, Robert, 109
Handedness, 52
Harold, 210–1
Harvard University, 40, 48
Harvey, Paul, 117
Hawthorne, Nathaniel, 62
Haymond, Tom, 129
Hearing. See Ear; Sound versus sight
Herbert, George, 61
Heroic females and males, 118–9
Holland, Josiah G., 163
Home Depot, 24, 84
Horizontal scheduling, 127–8, 130, 226
House account, 226
Hubbard, Elbert, 169
Huebner, Jim, 36–38, 60, 104, 138, 160, 178, 216
Hughes, Rupert, 199
Humor in advertising, 112, 113

Iacocca, Lee, 34
Iconic memory, 54–55, 93
Ideals, 196
Identity, 214–5
Illegal activities, 162–3
Illumination versus lighting, 140–1
Imagination
    active voice and, 115
    and creation of reality, 60, 65
    Dickinson on, 65
    engagement of, 44–45, 64–65, 117
    Adam Smith on, 46–47
    sympathy and, 46–47
Impact quotient (IQ), 105, 106
Inquiry into the Nature and Causes of the Wealth of Nations (Smith), 46–47
Inside champions, selling to, 18–21
Instant gratification, desire for, 156–7
Intellect versus emotion, 82–83, 168
Intellectual ads, 77, 83
Inventory turnover ratio, 146, 150–1
IQ (impact quotient), 105, 106
Irvine, Andrew, 161

Jaws, 82
Jeff, 210–1
Jefferson, Thomas, 46–47, 186, 187, 199
Jewelry, 88–89, 108, 118–9, 141–2
Jewish celebration, 214
Jobim, Antonio Carlos, 110
Johnny Appleseed, 194–5
Johnson, Phil, 63, 83
Journal of Cognitive Neuroscience, 48, 116
Journalism, 114, 115
Justice, Woody, 118

Kahneman, Daniel, 90, 172–3
Kentucky Fried Chicken (KFC), 24, 182
Kessler, Richard, 160
KFC. See Kentucky Fried Chicken (KFC)
Kipling, Rudyard, 13
Kitchen, V. C., 175
Knauth, Percy, 62
Kocurek, Maureen, 164
Kocurek, Willie, 164–5, 166
Kosslyn, Stephen, 48

La Rochefoucauld, François de, 69
Lady's Rolexes, 118–9
Landau, Martin, 28
Last mental image (LMI), 116–7
Learning
    Cicero on, 193
    from experience, 180
    from mistakes, 181
    by stopping and looking, 192–3
Lederer, William, 218–20
Leisure time, 33
Leonardo da Vinci, 59
Leprechaun, 202, 203
Letters of a Nation (Carroll), 218
Lighting, 140–1
Linage, 226
Lincoln, Abraham, 62, 186, 187, 199
Lincoln, James F., 171
Lincoln Manufacturing, 182–3
LMI. See Last mental image (LMI)
Long-range planning, 125
Long-term versus short-term advertising, 96–97, 126
Loss, fear of, 90–91
Loyalty, 216
Luck, 200–1
Lucky Charms, 202

M.A.S.H., 74
Maddock, Chris, 168
"Magic square," 58–59

as more important than facts, 40–41
Frank Lloyd Wright on, 40–41
Tugs-of-war
    intellect versus emotion, 82–83, 168
    opportunity versus security, 86–87
    pain versus gain, 90–91
    sight versus sound, 92–94
    style versus substance, 88–89
    time versus money, 84–85
Turnover of working capital ratio, 146
TV advertising, 96–97, 99, 107, 109, 116–7, 130–1
Tversky, Amos, 90, 172–3

Uncle Sam, 195
Unique selling proposition (USP), 28, 133
Unit pricing, 229
United Kingdom, 88–89
U.S. Junior Chamber of Commerce, 162
U.S. Trust, 32
Universal Knowledge Theory, 192, 193, 206, 207
University of Chicago, 90
Urgency, 156–7
USP. *See* Unique selling proposition (USP)

Vail, Theodore N., 211
Verbs, 52, 53, 110–1, 115
Vertical scheduling, 128, 229
Visual association area of brain, 50, 51
Visual cortex of brain, 50, 51
Voltaire, 76

War of 1812, 195
Washington, George, 186, 190–1
Wealth
    characteristics and needs of wealthy, 32–33
    philanthropy and, 202–3
    Adam Smith on, 46–47
    time versus money, 84–85
Wendy's Hamburgers, 34, 182
Wernicke, Carl, 50
Wernicke's area, 50, 51, 52, 70
White, Anthony Marc, 14–15
Wilde, 207
Wilde, Oscar, 206–7
Williams, Pennie, 14, 29, 85, 88, 164, 210, 212, 236
Williams, Roy Hollister
    biographical information on, 236
    coin collecting by, 200–1
    encounter with police officer, 14–15
    motorcycle accident of, 212–3
    and posting bail for neighbor, 210–1
    reading by, in childhood, 192, 217
    speaking engagements of, 68–69, 88–89

youth of, 18, 26, 217
Wilson, Betsey, 194, 195
Wilson, John M., 179
Wilson, Sam, 194
Wisdom, 135
Wizard of Ads (Williams), 36, 68, 132–3
Word-of-mouth advertising, 16, 128, 129
Words. *See also* Writing ad copy
    action words, 52–53, 110–1
    audacious words, 111
    energy of, 12–13, 83, 213
    "hearing" of, while reading, 48, 54–55
    mental images and, 70–71, 73, 91, 116–9
    unpredictable words in poetry, 72–73, 115
    unusual words in ads, 77
    verbs, 52, 53, 110–1
Wortman, Gary, 160
Wreck of the Titan (Robertson), 57
Wright, Frank Lloyd, 40–41
Wright, Wilbur, 87
Writing ad copy
    active versus passive voice for, 111
    and APE (advertising performance equation), 105, 106
    audacious words, 111
    drama in, 112, 113
    humor in, 112, 113
    mental images and, 116–9
    musical jingles, 74–75, 76, 77, 92, 112, 113
    and passion for own business, 102–3
    for print media, 108, 109
    for radio, 108–9
    testimonials and, 112, 113
    verbs in, 53, 110–1, 115
    "you" used in, 79

Yellow Pages, 96
"You" in ad copy, 79
Young, John, 80–81

Zimmer, George, 34

About the Wizard

Roy H. Williams, a contemplative observer by inclination and habit, has been a lifelong student of the human race, forever seeking to answer the question "What makes people do the things they do?"

Roy indulges his fascination with the future and the past by reading science fiction and historical biographies. He writes poetry, advertising, and screenplays. He's a riveting public speaker, but hates to travel: "On the third morning away from Pennie, I wake up with a cold sore on my lip. Maybe when the boys are older, she can travel with me and I won't be so miserable."

A collector of antiques and old books, pocket watches, fountain pens, vintage photographs, and automotive memorabilia, Roy is a self-described "pack rat." (Pennie agrees.) They have two sons, Rex and Jake.

Roy H. Williams Marketing, Inc., headquartered near Austin, Texas, creates controversial ad campaigns for small business clients in thirty-eight states. The firm occasionally hosts advertising seminars that are attended by business owners and students from around the world.

For additional copies of

Secret Formulas

of

the Wizard of Ads

$16.95 paperback
$26.95 hardcover

or

The Wizard of Ads

Turning Words into Magic and Dreamers into Millionaires

$16.95 paperback
$26.95 hardcover

visit your favorite bookstore

or call toll-free

1-800-945-3132

or fax your order to

512-288-5055.

Visa / MasterCard / Discover / American Express accepted.
Quantity discounts are available.

Bard Press

512-329-8373 voice
512-329-6051 fax
www.bardpress.com

Subscribe to the Monday Morning Memo at no charge by visiting www.WizardofAds.com